Human Rights

BUYER BEWARE

HUMAN RIGHTS

BUYER BEWARE

Safeguarding Consumer Rights

written by

Binah Taylor

Rourke Corporation, Inc.
Vero Beach, Florida 32964

Cover design: David Hundley

Library of Congress Cataloging-in-Publication Data
Taylor, Binah Brett, 1951-
    Buyer beware: safeguarding consumer rights / by Binah
Brett Taylor.
        p.   cm. — (Human rights)
    Includes bibliographical references and index.
    Summary: Examines consumer rights and discusses
how they are protected by law in such areas as food, drugs,
transportation, and toys.
    ISBN 0-86593-172-0 (alk. paper)
    1. Consumer protection — Law and legislation — United
States — Juvenile literature.   [1. Consumer protection —
Law and legislation.]   I. Title.   II. Series: Human
rights (Vero Beach, Fla.)
KF1610.T39   1992   92-5493
343.73'071 — dc20   CIP
[347.30371]   AC

Contents

Human Rights

BUYER BEWARE

Chapter One

What
Are
Consumer Rights?

To *consume* is to buy or to use something. Whether it is food, clothing, cars, appliances, toys, housing, or insurance, everyone is involved in consuming on a daily basis. Modern consumers have the potential to live in a world of marvels: They can eat tropical fruit in the midst of winter, thanks to improved methods of shipping fruit across the world; they can vacation in Bali and casually pay with a credit card; they can enjoy warm homes in a cold winter, thanks to gas piped in from miles away; and they can fax an important document to another country within minutes. Anyone who has ever purchased a product or a service is a *consumer*.

The Right to Safety

Consumers are entitled to products that do what they have been advertised to do, that are safe, and that have been tested for quality. Consumer rights are concerned with protecting consumers in these ways, and have come to be considered part of everyone's human rights. Even though in the short run laws protecting consumer rights help the buyer, ultimately these laws also serve the seller, because without satisfied buyers, a seller's livelihood is in jeopardy.

Safety is the most important aspect of consumer rights. Consumers want to know that the food they eat is free from pesticide residues and harmful bacteria; that the toys their children play with are not dangerous; and that equipment and appliances function safely and are not made from toxic materials. Consumers also want to be sure that the cars they drive can operate dependably under a wide variety of driving conditions. They want the air they breathe and the water they drink to be healthful.

The Right to Information

In order to have these things, consumers need information about the products they use. This means that a manufacturer must tell the truth about its product — about how and where it is made and about what it does and does not do. The price of the product should also be stated clearly, so that consumers are not confused into thinking something is cheaper than it really is. For example, if two boxes of detergent are different sizes but the same price, the consumer may be led to believe that the detergent in the bigger box is the better buy, even though the amount of both products may be the same by weight.

The right to be informed can also include truth in lending; that is, when consumers buy something on credit, the lender is obliged to tell them how much the interest charges will be, to list the conditions of the contract (such as liability), and to reveal how much they will pay overall. The Truth-in-Lending Act of 1968 was designed to protect consumers in credit transactions.

Even for those consumers who live in a democracy — where citizens expect, and even take for granted, that their human rights will be protected — not everyone, in practice, has equal access to the protection of laws against defective products. Members of minority races, minors (children), the elderly, the poor, and women are at a disadvantage because they have less power economically and in the legal system.

The Consumer Rights Movement

During the 1960's, lawmakers began to place special emphasis on consumer rights (although laws to ensure food safety were passed as early as the beginning of the twentieth century). This sudden burst of interest in consumer rights was largely the result of efforts by two early consumer rights activists: Rachel Carson, author of *Silent Spring* (1962), and Ralph Nader, author of *Unsafe at Any Speed* (1965). Carson's book addressed the issue of indiscriminate use of pesticides. As a result, the American consumer became wary of food

Ralph Nader, testifying before a Senate Commerce subcommittee in 1971, urged penalties for industry giants guilty of distributing dangerous products. (AP/Wide World Photos)

and water contaminated with pesticides and other chemicals. For the first time, consumers began to recognize the *interrelatedness* of all living things. Carson showed that what we do to the environment can affect not only consumers but the earth itself.

Nader's book on auto safety catapulted him to fame, but the event that established him as the principal spokesperson for consumers occurred a few years later at a 1968 Senate hearing on auto safety, when the president of General Motors was forced to admit that General Motors had investigated Nader's personal life because the company wanted to discredit him. Nader filed a suit against General Motors, which was settled out of court in his favor. In taking on such a giant and winning, Nader became a hero to millions of American consumers. The action of General Motors also served to sway congressional opinion in favor of the National Traffic and Motor Vehicle Safety Act of 1966, which established mandatory safety standards for automobiles and for new and used tires. The publicity around this event also made many Americans realize that businesses were not always working with consumer interests in mind. Nader and his group of consumer advocates, which came to be known as "Nader's Raiders," challenged many other businesses and did much to bring about the consumer protection laws that are enjoyed today.

As the consumer protection issue gained momentum in the early 1960's, politicians realized that it was to their advantage to become involved. President John F. Kennedy decided to take a front-line approach to consumer rights and in a message to Congress, on March 15, 1962, said:

> If consumers are offered inferior products, if prices are exorbitant, if drugs are unsafe or worthless, if the consumer is unable to choose on an informed basis, then his dollar is wasted, his health and safety may be threatened, and the national interest suffers.

Kennedy outlined four important aspects of consumer rights: (1) the right to safety, (2) the right to be informed, (3) the right to choose, and (4) the right to be heard. The consumer movement has added a fifth right: the right to recourse and redress — that is, the right to a fair settlement of claims.

Public Interest

Though there is much to be done, consumers today do have a voice and are protected by many more laws than there were in the 1960's. This improvement in protections can largely be attributed to the efforts of Nader and other consumer rights activists in creating public pressure for legislation.

Nader started a "public interest research group" (PIRG) in 1970, using his own funds. The purpose of this PIRG was to focus on lobbying rather than research. Nader and his colleagues would go to college and university campuses to encourage students to become active in the consumer movement, speaking on issues of justice, safety, equity, and environmental protection. By 1987, twenty-four PIRGs were operating in the United States. These PIRGs attracted criticism from the public for their coercive recruiting methods, but they were nevertheless effective in many areas, such as lobbying to clean up toxic wastes.

In 1987, the Consumer Federation of America — the largest consumer advocacy organization in the country, based in Washington, D.C. — estimated that there were more than two million members of state and local consumer groups. There are also some four million subscribers to *Consumer Reports*, a monthly magazine, published by Consumers Union of the United States, that reviews product quality and safety.

Another consumer advocate who is a public figure because of his television show, *Fight Back!*, is consumer reporter David Horowitz. His focus is consumer complaints and truth in

Consumers need information in order to make sound decisions. (The Image Works)

advertising, and his hallmark is product testing. His work has sometimes brought about changes in the system. In 1987, he was held at gunpoint with a realistic toy gun. Apart from the scare tactics of holding up someone in this manner — a violation of individual human rights and an act of assault — there can be fatal repercussions if the person held up fires at the assailant in self-defense with a real gun. This episode prompted state and federal legislation banning the sale of such toys.

Consumers vs. Sellers

Sellers and buyers are not always in battle with each other. In reality, sellers need consumers, and consumers need sellers. However, sellers do not often welcome laws to protect consumers, since they believe that such restrictions may not be to their advantage in the marketplace.

One of the reasons for tensions between buyers and sellers is the growth of markets throughout the world. The development of marketing has made more goods available, with a greater choice for consumers, but it has also resulted in an increase in deceptive marketing practices that has not served consumers. Among the difficulties sellers in the United States face is competition from manufacturers in Third World countries and rising costs at home. This is a complex issue, made worse when neither sellers nor consumers know enough about the safety of the product. Both sellers and consumers benefit when thorough research has been done on a product and both sides are educated as to its function and safety.

Chapter Two

Who Needs Consumer Rights?

In the United States, the Constitution and its amendments contain many protections for civil rights and liberties. Why, then, is it important to pass laws that deal specifically with *consumer* rights?

The field of consumer rights identifies and brings together the many problems that one very large and important group, consumers, face when they buy and use products. When the Constitution was drafted, there was neither the technology nor the variety of products available today. Its basic laws are far too broad and general to address all the specific infringements of human rights that may affect special groups of people, including consumers.

A Historical Overview

Consumers have risked being short-changed from the moment sellers and buyers got together: The old Roman saying *Caveat emptor* (which means "Buyer, beware") reveals an ancient and long-standing attitude that all may not be fair in the marketplace. Other than offering their repeat business, consumers have little control over manufacturing and pricing. Sellers who want to engage in a business for only a short while and make as much profit as they can have not worried about whether consumers are satisfied or safe.

During the 1960's, public awareness of consumer rights increased; however, the need for consumer rights was not new to the American public. Concern over consumer protection had emerged at the beginning of the twentieth century, after a period of intense production in a sellers' market. During this period, many inferior goods were sold. Food in particular was doctored to help the seller, not the buyer.

Without consumer legislation, it was acceptable for a seller to add formaldehyde to milk or to color candy with poisonous aniline dye. According to Hamilton P. Duffield, in his article "The Adulteration of Food and Medicine" (*The Making of America*, 1905), these additives, while not powerful enough to cause death, nevertheless endangered the health of the consumer. A group of consumers decided to band together to do something about this problem, and in 1891 the Consumers League was formed in New York; it was expanded and renamed the National Consumers' League in 1898. By 1906, the Pure Food and Drug Act — the first measure to guard against unsafe foods, including additives — was passed by Congress, and consumer protection in the United States was born.

When the Great Depression struck in the 1930's, several books were published about how the consumer is endangered in the marketplace. One such book was Arthur Kallet and F. J. Schlink's *100,000,000 Guinea Pigs* (1933), which was an indictment of how companies expose consumers to untested products. The book was a best-seller and helped to bring about the Federal Food, Drug, and Cosmetic Act of 1938.

Between 1938 and the 1960's, little consumer legislation passed Congress. Then, in the 1960's, laws began to be passed to ensure that drugs were tested before they were put on themarket. The same period saw hearings in government about auto safety; subsequent legislation required manufacturers to build cars with more safety features, such as seat belts. Increased auto safety became a continuing process, and every few years there was some new invention on the market to make cars safer for drivers and passengers. By the 1990's, driver and even passenger air bags were becoming standard features in many new cars.

Despite increased consumer awareness in the 1960's, consumers were still at risk. In 1975, for example, Senator Birch Bayh from Indiana stated that about 20 percent of the accidental deaths and injuries in America during 1974 may have been related to household consumer products. Since the 1980's, there has been growing concern among consumer watchdogs that the trend toward deregulation of industries (reduction of governmental controls on how companies conduct their businesses), which began during President Reagan's administration, has resulted in a decline of standards and less protection for consumers.

Today, consumers have some means of knowing whether a product will last and whether they paid the right price for it. Brand names that have a consistently good record offer one way to be assured, but it is even more reassuring to know that there will be a money-back guarantee if the product does not work. It is also reassuring to know that the product has been thoroughly tested for safety and quality before being put on the market. These are some of the protections available to consumers now.

Nevertheless, the setbacks of the 1980's have made it difficult for government regulating agencies to catch and discipline sellers who ignore these protections. It is up to consumers to know their rights, to exercise their rights, and to lobby for more rights when existing laws prove to be inadequate. The old saying "Buyer, beware" is still good advice.

Truth in Advertising?

No industrialized country matches the United States in amount of money spent on advertising. Advertising on television or on the package can mislead the consumer into thinking that the product will do more than, or something different from, what it actually does.

Action for Children's Television (ACT) is a consumer interest group which monitors commercials on television with regard to children's health and safety. At Senate hearings in 1973, ACT raised the issue of the quality of food products (such as cereal) being advertised on television. Two years before, ACT had filed petitions with the FTC to ban from children's television programming commercials about food and toys. ACT alleged that all food advertising aimed at children was misleading because it encouraged them to put pressure on their parents to buy food low in nutrition. These charges were not entirely successful, although the National Association of Broadcasting (NAB) reduced commercial time for children on weekends by 25 percent.

Advertising on television has also been restricted for alcohol and tobacco. This ban once included antismoking campaigns that were waged on television. Since the 1980's, however, antidrug campaigns have returned to television. For a time there was a ban on comparative advertising, such as "Folgers is better than MJB," but this ban was lifted in 1972.

Another group susceptible to television advertising is the elderly, because they watch a lot of television. The elderly have a limited budget and also a strong need, like children, for nutritious food. The American Association of Retired Persons (AARP) is concerned that the elderly are not eating enough nutritious food because they are influenced by the food advertising on television, most of which encourages people to buy heavily processed food with inadequate nutritional content.

The old Roman saying "Buyer, beware" suggests that not all deals may be as good as they seem. (Uniphoto)

Who Is At Risk?

Not all consumers enjoy the same rights, and the poor —
those whose incomes fall near or below the poverty line — may
well be at the greatest disadvantage. In his book *The Poor Pay
More* (1963), David Caplovitz showed that the poor are the
main victims of overcharging, deceptive advertising, and
dangerous merchandise. Because they also find it harder to get
credit, they are often forced to go to lenders who charge higher
fees and rates.

One of the biggest problems faced by poor consumers is
access: to good products, good prices, and good protection.
Poor neighborhoods may offer few or no supermarkets but
only small grocery stores with restricted choices and costlier
goods. As many of the poor do not have access to cars and
may have to wait hours for public transportation, getting to the
less expensive outlets for food and other goods may be
impossible, given the time available. This leaves many poor
persons with little choice but to go to the local store and pay
the higher prices. To complicate matters, many of these poor
represent racial or ethnic minority groups in the United
States — African Americans, Hispanics, or Asians. When the
poor members of these groups also suffer a language barrier, it
is even harder for them to learn and implement their rights or
to have a voice in the legal system.

Ethnicity presents another problem that adversely affects
poor consumers' rights: discrimination. African Americans, for
example, have for generations been discriminated against in
many ways — including as consumers. In the first suit of its
kind, Charles and Janice Tyler of Illinois won a court case in
1969 in which they filed charges that, as potential home
buyers, they were not shown certain houses because Charles
Tyler was an African American. Several months after they had
moved, the house they had bought was burned down, and
arson was suspected. African Americans, as well as Hispanics

and Asians, still experience this type of discrimination all over the United States. With lax enforcement of anti-discrimination laws since the 1980's, consumer discrimination based on race has unfortunately not decreased.

The elderly, too, are consumers who are discriminated against in a number of ways, but especially when it comes to buying medical insurance. Many of the elderly are not eligible for affordable insurance rates; because they are older, the risk of their having to make expensive claims is, of course, much higher. Worse, some insurance companies will refuse to insure them, citing "pre-existing conditions." This is also the situation for those who have tested positive for the AIDS virus or who have full-blown AIDS. By the 1990's, some life insurance companies were allowing their customers to cash in their life insurance policies to help pay for the high medical costs that result from AIDS treatment.

Children and young adults are another subgroup who suffer as consumers. Children are very impressionable; naturally trusting of what they see or hear, they can easily be persuaded to want toys and food advertised on television. Television commercials also target young adults, luring them to purchase goods that promise to deliver a more exciting (often, a more sexually exciting) life. Flashy images of parties and attractive young people, for example, are designed to sell everything from fast food to alcoholic beverages. Teenagers also experience a form of discrimination similar to that faced by older persons: Because young drivers are statistically more likely to have automobile accidents, they are forced to pay extremely high rates for car insurance. The pressures that this imposes on young adults who must have transportation for work and school may even encourage them to drive without insurance, which makes the problem worse. Finally, young people live in a society that requires a credit history in order to make major purchases and pay for them over a period of time.

It is difficult to get credit without a credit history, so most young adults have to rely on their parents as co-signers.

These are some of the consumer subgroups who experience less freedom than the average person in the United States. The disadvantaged consumer can benefit from specialized consumer advocate groups in order to use the democratic system and bring about change.

Groups for All Reasons

Consumer rights groups came into being once consumers began to recognize their plight and the need to organize as a group. By making the public aware of consumer problems and by demanding that manufacturers and sellers adhere to certain standards of quality and honesty, consumer rights activists have strengthened consumer rights in a way that would not have been possible if consumers had individually invoked their rights under the Constitution.

One of the first consumer rights groups was the Consumers League, formed about one hundred years ago. It was this group that made people aware of such injustices as unsafe working conditions and child labor, as well as long hours for small wages.

Some consumer protection organizations — such as Ralph Nader's Public Citizen, Consumer Federation of America, the Conference of Consumer Organizations, and the National Consumer League — deal with all kinds of consumer issues, everything from defective products to truth in advertising. Other groups, such as the Group Against Smokers' Pollution (GASP) and Action for Children's Television (ACT), focus on a single consumer interest.

Just how effective a consumer interest group can be is shown by the AARP. This organization lobbied successfully to get cheaper medication for retired people. Through their efforts, senior citizens can now get generic (non-brand) prescription drugs from pharmacies in most states, and the number of pharmacies offering generic drugs is growing. These generic drugs are chemically identical to their brand-name counterparts, but significantly less expensive. Since a large proportion of the older population depends on these medicines to maintain a normal life, they are often at the mercy of large drug companies that charge many times the price of manufacturing the drugs — unless generic equivalents are available.

Sometimes the most unlikely groups will come together for a common cause. At one antinuclear rally in Washington, D.C., the Communist Party, the International Association of Machinists, the Union of Concerned Scientists, and the Clamshell Alliance all joined forces. On the other side of the coin, consumer groups can often rally around opposing sides of the same issue: Conflicting consumer attitudes toward firearms can be seen in pro-handgun groups, such as the National Rifle Association, and anti-handgun groups, such as Handgun Control, based in Washington, D.C.

In addition to private organizations, consumer groups come in the guise of government agencies. However, consumer advocates have become disillusioned with government agencies, such as the Consumer Product Safety Commission and the National Highway Traffic Safety Administration, because they move so slowly and take so long to bring about change. Consumers have also charged that so-called policing agencies such as the Better Business Bureau sometimes act in the interests of business before acting in the interests of consumers. Nader has said that dealing with government agencies can be worse than dealing with the businesses he opposes. Along with other consumer advocates, he believes that the class action suit is a powerful tool for the consumer. A class action suit is a legal action taken by a group of people, who all have the same complaint, against a person or organization that they believe has compromised their rights.

Setting Priorities

Today in the United States, there are six areas in which consumers need special help. All of them are areas essential to life, and all of them are a result of the higher cost of living:

(1) The high cost of food.
(2) Rising medical costs, including the high cost of health insurance.
(3) High costs in housing, for both buying and renting.
(4) Higher costs of cars and auto insurance.
(5) Lower quality of merchandise or products, which results in high repair costs.

Chapter Three

Food

Some of the earliest legislation in the United States to protect consumers targeted the quality of food that people eat. In 1906, the Pure Food and Drug Act was passed. This bill came about because of proven allegations that imitation foods were — unbeknownst to consumers — being sold as real foods. The bill was also passed to protect farmers whose markets were being invaded by the cheaper substitutes. In 1906, the Meat Inspection Act was also passed, in part as a result of the bad publicity generated by Upton Sinclair's book, *The Jungle*, which exposed the unsanitary conditions of the meat-packing houses in Chicago.

What's the Law?

After the flurry of concern about the quality of food in the early twentieth century, there was no further legislation until the 1930's. The Federal Food, Drug, and Cosmetic Act of 1938 amended the 1906 act, and the Food Additives Amendment of 1958, also known as the Delaney Amendment, in turn amended the 1938 act. The Delaney Amendment stated that only foods not known to cause cancer in humans or animals would be recognized as safe. One of the limitations of the Food Additives Amendment of 1958 was that it referred only to additives that cause cancer; it did not include additives that can cause birth deformities.

Further controls came about with the Hazardous Substances Labeling Act of 1960, which regulated the labeling of packages

hoppers can compare food labels of similar items to make an informed choice. (Bob
)aemmrich/The Image Works)

of hazardous household substances, and the Wholesome Poultry Products Act of 1968, which required state inspections of poultry for bacteria, such as salmonella, to meet federal standards.

The idea that what people eat is of public concern and should be controlled by law is new in the United States. Developing countries generally have more legislation about what people eat because in those countries there has historically been more risk of poor nutrition and disease.

Food Testing and the FDA

What people eat has a big impact on their health. This makes food a strong target for consumer activists, who are trying to protect consumers. Sometimes it is very difficult to establish whether or not a food is dangerous. In the 1970's, the Food and Drug Administration (FDA) put at the top of its list of priorities monitoring the side effects of medicinal drugs. Critics argued that food free from toxins should be the priority, because everyone eats food.

When manufacturers propose new foods for the marketplace, the food has to undergo years of rigorous testing before finally winning (or not winning) approval from the FDA. An example is aspartame, also known by its brand-name, Nutrasweet. After more than ten years of testing, it was placed on the market, and it quickly established itself as the number-one sugar substitute. It will be interesting to see if in twenty years aspartame will be as highly regarded as a food sweetener as it is today. Any food that is on the FDA's GRAS ("generally recognized as safe") list, which currently includes aspartame, could change its status in the future.

Sickeningly Sweet?

Artificial sweeteners are of concern to health-watch experts because they are so freely used. The National Academy of

Sciences has estimated that 75 percent of the U.S. public use some form of sugar substitute.

Saccharin, also known as a cyclamate, was freely available on the market and was used by dieters and diabetics alike in sweetening food and drink, until evidence surfaced in 1969 that large amounts of cyclamates could cause cancer in animals. In 1970, the FDA required all food products containing cyclamates to be removed from the market. This regulation took some time to go into effect, and the delay, with its potential hazards to consumers, caused a great debate. In 1972, the FDA removed saccharin from the GRAS list. By 1977, the Saccharin Study and Labeling Act required a health warning on products containing saccharin. However, the ban on saccharin was postponed in 1977. Today, saccharin is available on the market; it can be found, for example, in some diet colas.

The "flavor enhancer" monosodium glutamate, also known as MSG, is another controversial substance. There was a similar dispute between the consumer rights activist Ralph Nader and the FDA over the safety of MSG. According to Nader, consumers were led to believe that MSG was safe even though members of the scientific community were not in agreement over its safety. The FDA took no action to ban MSG, though three American baby food producers banned the flavor enhancer after a scientist had linked MSG to brain damage in infant mice. MSG continues to be sold in many packaged foods, especially soups and noodle mixes, as well as canned and frozen foods. Some people claim to get headaches after they eat foods prepared with MSG.

The beef industry has come under fire for indiscriminately using hormones and antibiotics on animals. The concern is that these substances, when eaten in meat, can interfere with the immune system, as well as with the endocrine (hormone) system. The U.S. House Government Operations Committee charged the FDA in 1986 with failing to test and approve 90 percent of the drugs given to animals by farmers and veterinarians.

Unfortunately, it is impossible for the FDA to monitor all new (and old) developments in food and drugs in such a diverse and extensive marketplace. Thus, while the FDA needs to improve its ability to do its job, consumers need more information about what they are eating.

Nutritional Education

The average consumer is usually not well informed about which foods are nutritious. That situation is changing as good health and nutrition habits are being taught in schools and colleges; the hope is that future adult consumers will be more informed.

In general, the more processed a food is (the more cooking, pulverizing, and other preparation goes into its production), the more it is exposed to additives and processing methods that can reduce its nutritional value or even render it unsafe. Reading food labels is important in order to become familiar with what additives have been used and what warning labels (if any) say.

Any person who falls into a high-risk group — such as pregnant and nursing mothers or individuals with unusual health conditions, such as diabetes or allergies — should consume questionable foods and chemicals, such as caffeine, in moderation or preferably not at all. Even "natural" foods such as whole fruits and vegetables go through some processing, if one considers the use of pesticides. A 1987 report by the National Academy of Sciences raised the possibility that pesticides on food may be responsible for 20,000 cancers per year in the United States. Washing all fruits and vegetables before eating them is recommended, because small amounts of pesticides, as well as bacteria, may be on their skins.

The Mouths of Babes

Babies are one of the highest-risk groups of consumers when it comes to food, because the infant body is not yet developed to protect itself as well as the adult body. Yet there was little public policy regarding nutritional needs of children and infants until the 1960's. At that time, physicians and health workers in developing countries believed that commercial infant foods manufactured for consumers in industrialized nations were being promoted to people who could not use them — at least not without risk to health. It was discovered that mothers living in poverty and unhygienic conditions were using contaminated water sources (often the only water available) to mix formula. When the formula was fed to their babies, the children became sick and sometimes died.

By the 1970's there were strained relations between pediatricians — who were trying to promote breast-feeding of infants as the better source of milk for the first year of life — and big formula companies, such as Nestlé, who were selling formula in many countries, including the Third World. By 1975, the International Pediatrics Association had endorsed breast-feeding as the medically superior method to feed infants. During a lawsuit against Nestlé in Switzerland, the public heard many charges against this company. Consumer activists who were advocating for better-quality, nonhazardous food for people organized a boycott against foods made by Nestlé. The dispute was finally settled in 1984, and by then Nestlé had changed its policy on marketing infant formula. The 1980 Infant Formula Act rules that formula manufacturers must state on the product that breast-milk is the preferred milk source for infants for the first year of life.

Public attention to the nutrition of infants has extended to older children as well. The National School Lunch Act was passed to ensure that school-age children receive hot, nourishing meals that meet their nutritional needs. Yet a study completed in 1981 of a sample of seven school systems in the United States, all using different lunch menus, showed that none of them met the goal of providing one-third of a teenager's recommended daily allowance (or RDA, established by the FDA under the guidelines of a 1973 regulation on food labeling). This nutritionally inadequate lunch program was an example of the government acting as a seller and not meeting consumers' needs. In effect, the federal government had acted as a marketer, requiring that schools buy and prepare food that did not actually meet their consumers' (the children's) needs.

Pregnant women are another high-risk group: They have greater nutritional needs and their unborn babies are also vulnerable to the ill effects of whatever their mothers may consume. It is only in the late 1980's that warning signs were placed in liquor stores, declaring that alcohol consumption during pregnancy can cause birth defects and other complications, including fetal alcohol syndrome. Caffeine is a substance that has been linked with certain side effects in infants who were exposed during their gestation. Caffeine is present in many popular products, not just coffee and tea; it is consumed in large amounts in colas and other sodas. However, no regulation requires a label to warn pregnant women, nursing mothers, or children about the dangers of consuming caffeine.

Food and Advertising

The relationship between food advertising and nutrition has become a major public issue. A number of consumer activists and activist groups, including Ralph Nader, Action for Children's Television (ACT), and the Center for Science in the Public Interest, have criticized food manufacturers for marketing their foods in a way that promotes poor dietary habits among Americans.

Food commercials make up the major portion of advertising on television, and a significant number of foods advertised on television have a high sugar content. In addition, a large proportion of food advertising is aimed at children, who have a limited ability to determine what is nutritionally sound. In response to concerns about the influence of television on children, ACT was formed to push for legislation to protect children by reducing commercial time on television during their peak viewing period. In England, for example, television is not allowed to run food commercials aimed at children when programs for children are aired. In the United States, the Federal Trade Commission (FTC) proposed in the 1970's that television advertising aimed at children be banned. Although this proposal fell through, pressure from ACT succeeded in restricting food advertising during children's peak viewing hours.

An example of how powerful television can be is illustrated by an ad campaign for Kellogg's Frosted Flakes. In 1985, this cereal ousted General Mills' Cheerios as the top-selling breakfast cereal. Cheerios had been advertised on the slogan of "only one gram of sugar per serving," but Tony the Tiger's sugar-coated flakes surpassed it in sales, because children had heard for years how "grrreat" they were. The result was that children pressed their parents to buy the cereal for them. The parents then learned to prefer it, too. Now ads for Frosted Flakes are targeted at the adults who learned to like the cereal as children.

Pest-Free or Poison?

Consumer protection advocates, as well as environmentalists, have tracked the use of pesticides on crops. Pesticides not only are potentially hazardous to the environment but also may be found in the food itself. Pesticides can therefore endanger consumers who eat the food, as well as farm workers who are exposed to the pesticides in the fields. César Chávez, the leader of California's farm workers, rallied support for consumers to boycott California table grapes, when he underwent a public fast in 1988 to protest the high levels of pesticides commonly used on this fruit.

Pesticides, like food additives or drugs, have been tested and then put on the market after meeting a government agency's approval. Nevertheless, some pesticides considered safe have later been found to be hazardous. The pesticide DDT, widely used both commercially and privately throughout the United States, was found after testing to be unsafe. Federal regulations in 1969 banned further production of DDT, which had contaminated birds, fish, and other wildlife. Unfortunately, manufacturers of DDT found ways to sell this pesticide in other countries, such as Mexico, where it continued to be used on crops.

Pesticide residues may remain on fruits and vegetables. (U.S. Department of Agriculture)

Food Irradiation

A recent and ongoing controversy is over food irradiation. When food is *irradiated*, it is exposed to a cobalt ray. Supporters of food irradiation cite its advantages: The ray kills harmful bacteria such as salmonella, which poses a danger to consumers, particularly those who eat chicken and other poultry. Because irradiation eliminates bacteria, the food will not decompose, so it can stay on store shelves for a long time. Certain foods in Europe, such as potatoes and some meats, have been irradiated for years, and the World Health Organization (WHO) has given its approval of the process, considering food irradiation to be as important as pasteurization.

After examining a number of studies, the FDA approved food irradiation in 1986. In 1991, a consumer group against irradiated food opposed the opening of a food-irradiation plant in Florida, resulting in the opening being delayed indefinitely. The group so far has been successful in stopping irradiation of fish caught in Alaska and papayas from Hawaii. Their slogan is "Human life, not shelf life," and two of their arguments against irradiation are that it poses a cancer risk and can mask poor quality of food. There is also evidence that irradiating foods can diminish their vitamin A, C, and E content.

Food production and processing methods are much more streamlined and safety-conscious than they were at the beginning of the twentieth century, when the first food and drug act was passed. The growth of the food additive industry and the emphasis on convenience foods, however, make it crucial that consumer interest groups continue to put pressure on the FDA to monitor safety of food products and for the FTC to restrict deceptive food advertising on television.

Chapter Four

Alcohol, Drugs, and Tobacco

Alcohol, medicinal drugs (both prescribed and over-the-counter), and tobacco are widely used by many different people. These substances can be extremely dangerous and even lethal — especially to young people, whose bodies are still forming and whose lives can be ruined by misuse or abuse of these chemicals. It is unfortunate that casual attitudes toward drugs, particularly alcohol and tobacco, have been promoted on television and in films by a society that knows the risks.

It is therefore crucial that these substances be regulated for safety, health, and effectiveness. Consumer activists have put many pressures on Congress to ensure that controls are placed on the advertising of alcohol and tobacco. The Food and Drug Administration (FDA) was established to monitor the safety of food and drug consumption by the public; sometimes it has taken a consumer activist group or a class action suit to put pressure on the FDA to retest or recall a drug that is on the GRAS ("generally recognized as safe") list.

Prescription and Over-the-Counter Drugs

After the 1906 Pure Food and Drug Act, there were few laws protecting consumers until the Depression era, when the consumer interest again emerged and food and drug regulation was given priority. In 1934, the FDA unleashed a campaign called "The Chamber of Horrors," a series of posters that showed the ill effects on people — such as disfigurement, blindness, poisoning, and even death — caused by some unregulated drugs and cosmetics. In 1938, the Federal Food, Drug, and Cosmetic Act was finally passed by Congress. There were weaknesses in this bill that were amended in 1962 with the Kefauver-Harris Amendments.

These amendments require that a drug be proven effective before it can be sold to the public. Previously, a drug had to be safe but not necessarily effective. Critics of the 1962 amendments say that by requiring drugs to be proven effective, the new laws forced the price of drugs to go up and therefore have cost consumers many millions of dollars. Furthermore, the requirement that the FDA withhold drugs until they were proven effective, it was thought, cost some consumers their lives. This criticism was renewed in the 1980's, as an increasing number of AIDS sufferers waited for new drugs to be proven effective before they could have access to them. For many AIDS patients, with a limited time to live, the wait would prove to be too long; some attempted to procure the promising new drugs in other countries.

There are basically two ways that a drug can be regulated if it is on the market at all: by making it available only through a doctor's prescription, and by labeling it with any known side effects or circumstances under which it should not be taken. It is safer to ask about harmful side effects and to read labels before taking a drug. For example, taking a prescribed tranquillizer with alcohol can be fatal. Such drugs should never be used together, for they have a "potentiate" effect; that is, together they are more powerful than the sum of their separate effects. Smoking also adversely affects the assimilation of medication.

Even more dangerous, some drugs may not be compatible with driving. Many driver handbooks, available from most state departments of motor vehicles, include a warning sign requesting drivers to ask their physicians about medication and driving.

Side Effects

Harmful side effects from drugs pose a widespread problem. In the United States, more than one million people every year are hospitalized because of a bad reaction to a drug. About one-third of these hospitalizations occur as the result of taking over-the-counter drugs — drugs that practically anyone can purchase without the order of a doctor — and the rest are attributable to prescription drugs.

During the 1950's, thalidomide, a tranquillizer, was given to pregnant women in Europe to reduce nausea but was subsequently found to cause birth defects. Thalidomide babies, as they were called, typically were born with missing or deformed arms, legs, fingers, or toes. Americans narrowly missed mass marketing of thalidomide; fortunately, the side effects of the drug became known before the FDA approved it for over-the-counter distribution. A single FDA officer, Dr. Frances Kelsey, had insisted on further testing of the drug.

Sometimes a drug has passed safety regulations or is on the GRAS list, and then, after some years of availability on the market, exhibits side effects that arouse public concern. Aspirin, for example, is a widely used over-the-counter drug which, if frequently consumed, can cause bleeding of the stomach lining or stomach ulcers. On the other hand, aspirin has been prescribed to heart patients because of its ability to reduce the threat of heart attacks.

Acetaminophen (marketed under brand-names such as Tylenol) has been the preferred pain reliever for children and those sensitive to aspirin. Yet Tylenol, too, has had its

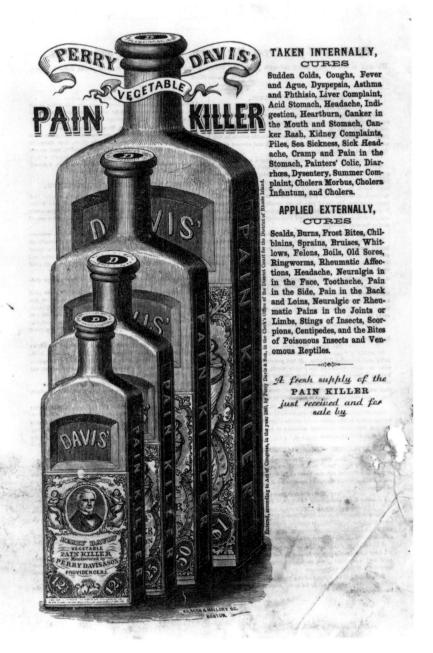

Before truth-in-advertising laws, some "medicines" made outlandish claims. (Library of Congress)

problems: In 1982, several people were murdered when someone placed the poison cyanide inside the Tylenol capsules. Within weeks, the federal government issued regulations that medicine bottles must be made tamper-proof.

The FDA's intent is to limit the risks of taking a drug without depriving those in need of medication. In 1972, in response to evidence that hexachlorophene (found in mouthwashes, toothpaste, and a soap marketed as Phisohex) was absorbed into the bloodstream, the FDA banned this substance in over-the-counter drugs. Those people who were using Phisohex because they had skin problems became alarmed and started stocking up on the product. In this instance, a sector of the public that had benefitted from the drug was deprived of its use.

Ineffective Drugs

In 1962, when the Kefauver-Harris Amendments were passed, there were many ineffective drugs on the market; in fact, a study conducted by the National Academy of Sciences found that 41 percent of FDA-approved drugs on the market between 1938 and 1962 were known to be ineffective in achieving at least one of its claimed benefits. According to a 1983 publication prepared by Public Citizen's Health Research Group, over-the-counter drugs such as some painkillers, mouthwashes, and hemorrhoid medications are too often "ineffective." These drugs are still on the market, which implies that the 1962 amendments have not been effective either.

Ineffective drugs not only rob consumers of their dollars but also jeopardize lives, because precious time is wasted during the use of the ineffective drug.

Tobacco and Its Hazards

Tobacco has been another controversial substance. Tobacco use, once widely accepted by the public and tolerated by public health agencies such as the FDA, is now considered a major hazard to public health. Tobacco was at one time a significant crop in the United States, and the tobacco companies had formidable power and influence.

Not only is the carbon monoxide from smoke hazardous, but nicotine in tobacco is highly addictive. Those who chew tobacco also are at risk of developing mouth cancers. Since 1985, cigarette packs have been labeled with the following warning:

> SURGEON GENERAL'S WARNING: SMOKING CAUSES LUNG CANCER, HEART DISEASE, EMPHYSEMA, AND MAY COMPLICATE PREGNANCY.

This is a considerable advance over the 1966 Cigarette Labeling Act, which required manufacturers to place a general health warning on cigarette packs.

The dangers of smoking during pregnancy continue to be documented. Figures in 1988 indicate that pregnant women who smoke have more miscarriages and more stillbirths than nonsmokers. Infants who have been exposed to smoking *in utero* have lower birth weights, and there is growing concern about negative effects on infants in terms of intellectual, emotional, and behavioral development. Young children are also at risk of severe nicotine poisoning, including death, should they ingest cigarette butts. Parents and adults should make sure that ashtrays are out of reach of children.

Antismoking Campaigns

In 1964, the U.S. Surgeon General made his first statement connecting ill health to smoking. Sweden was the first country to propose a long-term, coordinated program to educate the public on the health dangers of smoking. Their mandate was that no child born after 1975 would grow up to be a smoker.

In the United States, there are now laws in effect that either section off smokers in public places, such as restaurants, or do not allow smoking at all, such as on buses or short airline trips. Stricter legislation has come about as a result of intense lobbying of two antismoking groups: Action on Smoking and Health (ASH) and Group Against Smokers' Pollution (GASP). In its early years, ASH focused on reducing the number of smokers; later, the group's focus turned to the rights of nonsmokers.

Advertising of cigarettes and tobacco products on television has been prohibited since the 1970's. Initially this also hurt the antismoking groups, which could no longer advertise either. In the long term, however, the lack of television advertising has resulted in less smoking among the population. Tobacco products continue to be advertised on billboards and in print, but antismoking groups have also been active. Recent figures show that the government spends $2 million annually for

Percentages of Cigarette Smokers in the United States

	1965	1970	1974	1976	1977	1978	1979	1980	1983	1985	1987
Sex											
Male	50.2	44.3	43.4	42.1	40.9	39.0	38.4	38.5	35.5	33.2	31.5
Female	31.9	30.8	31.4	31.3	31.4	29.6	29.2	29.0	28.7	28.0	26.2
Race											
White	40.0	36.5	36.1	35.6	34.9	33.6	33.2	32.9	31.4	29.9	28.3
Black	43.0	41.4	44.0	41.2	41.8	38.2	36.8	37.2	36.6	36.0	33.5
Education											
H.S.	n/a	38.3	37.6	37.8	38.4	36.5	35.4	35.7	35.6	34.2	32.9
Col.	n/a	28.1	28.3	27.4	25.6	23.8	23.4	24.6	19.9	18.4	16.1

SOURCE: Data are from the U.S. Centers for Disease Control, Office of Smoking and Health, Atlanta, Georgia.
NOTES: "H.S." = high school graduate; "Col." = college graduate.

nonsmoking advertising. (Tobacco companies spend $3 million to promote their product.) In 1990, there was a powerful antismoking billboard campaign, in Spanish, in Southern California, designed to reach the Hispanic population. The billboards depicted a skeleton smoking and saying: "Yo muerto para fumar." ("I am dying to smoke.")

The antismoking momentum of the 1980's has also produced more stringent laws that require airlines to schedule no-smoking flights. By the late 1980's, a federally imposed smoking ban had been introduced on all domestic flights of two hours or less. This ban was later increased to include all domestic flights of five hours or less. The smoking ban on airplanes is due to consumer activist groups such as GASP and ASH, which lobbied Congress to pass legislation in an effort to reduce fire hazards posed by smoking in toilets on airplanes.

Alcohol: Legal and Lethal

Alcohol is another controversial substance in the United States, and has been since the Prohibition era during the 1920's and 1930's. Nevertheless, alcohol is probably the most widely used mood-altering substance in the United States, and the growth of groups such as Alcoholics Anonymous testifies to the fact that many Americans are not able to control their alcohol intake. Certain individuals, for example, are genetically sensitive to alcohol and have low tolerance for its effects. These individuals show a tendency for addiction to the drug.

Public policy in the United States has been slow to monitor alcohol intake but is now taking a much tougher stand, particularly with stricter penalties for drinking and driving. In most states, a driver is considered drunk if he or she has a blood alcohol concentration (BAC) of .10; in a few states, including California, Maine, Oregon, and Utah, the BAC is .08, which roughly breaks down to about two drinks per hour, depending on body weight. The level varies from state to state.

During 1989, there were 252,445 drunk and drugged driving convictions reported to state departments of motor vehicles nationwide. In California alone, some 250,000 driving arrests were related to alcohol during 1990. During that year, 50 percent of all traffic fatalities in the United States — some forty-six thousand — were alcohol-related.

In many states, it is illegal for anyone under twenty-one years of age to purchase or drink alcohol. The lobbying group Mothers Against Drunk Drivers (MADD), founded by Candy Lightner in 1980 after her daughter was killed by a drunk driver, has successfully encouraged Congress to place pressure on state and local governments and to strengthen their liquor laws and prosecute violations, such as failure to verify the age of a customer by requesting identification. Since the mid-1980's, all beverages that contain alcohol have the following warning:

> GOVERNMENT WARNING: (1) ACCORDING TO THE SURGEON GENERAL, WOMEN SHOULD NOT DRINK ALCOHOLIC BEVERAGES DURING PREGNANCY BECAUSE OF THE RISK OF BIRTH DEFECTS. (2) CONSUMPTION OF ALCOHOLIC BEVERAGES IMPAIRS YOUR ABILITY TO DRIVE A CAR OR OPERATE MACHINERY, AND MAY CAUSE HEALTH PROBLEMS.

Pregnant women who drink place their infants at risk for fetal alcohol syndrome, a disease that can cause brain impairment and learning disorders. Infants with fetal alcohol syndrome typically have a certain "look," notably a long upper lip and eyes set very wide apart.

Implants and Other Devices

Federal regulation of both prescription and non-prescription drugs can include such devices as implants. These are "foreign" substances that are placed inside the body and should meet safety standards — at least, that has been the FDA's aim. Since the early 1960's silicone implants have been on the market, and in 1976, when the FDA started regulating medical devices, implants were automatically approved, like many other products, with the understanding that manufacturers would have to document their safety later. With some 150,000 women in the United States receiving breast implants each year — 80 percent of whom are doing it for cosmetic reasons that do not result from cancer surgery — it is crucial that the safety of silicone in the body be established.

In January, 1992, FDA Commissioner David Kessler announced a temporary ban on silicone implants. This decision came in the wake of many allegations by dissatisfied consumers who experienced discomfort, pain, and medical side effects from the breast implants, including evidence of immunological disorders. In April, 1992, the FDA ruled against use of implants unless for reconstructive surgery. However, the FDA left the door open for cosmetic use of the implants by allowing women to get them if they agreed to participate in breast-implant research projects. An increasing number of lawsuits concerning silicone implants have been filed. Dow Corning, a leading silicone manufacturer, has continued to claim the safety of the implants. The company's internal memos, however, suggest that Dow Corning may have rushed the product to market in 1975.

The breast implant controversy is similar to a controversy that arose in the 1970's, that of the intrauterine contraceptive device known as the Dalkon Shield. Tens of thousands of women who used that device were found to be at risk of complications ranging from discomfort to pelvic inflammatory disease before the device was taken off the market.

Dentistry offers another area of concern over implant safety. The possibility that mercury fillings in teeth may pose a health hazard arose when researchers at the University of Iowa found that everyday chewing may release some of the mercury into

Teenagers see television commercials that glamorize drinking, but drinking alcohol can cause fatal accidents, addictions, and birth defects. (Wendy Eldis/Uniphoto)

the mouth. The American Dental Association (ADA) has said that fillings (which are composed of silver and other metals, such as mercury) are safe. An article in the April, 1990, issue of *The Journal of the American Dental Association* stated that, out of the billions of fillings given to patients, there have been only fifty known cases of allergic reaction since 1905.

The Burden of Responsibility

With so many drugs on the market, and with medical technology providing a growing variety of options such as implants, a heavy burden has fallen on regulatory agencies such as the FDA: They must make the technology available to those in need yet, at the same time, protect consumers from side effects. This makes it even more crucial for consumer interest groups to push for safety where the FDA is falling behind. Likewise, with alcohol and tobacco products — two legal drugs that are widely used for their mood-altering, not medicinal, effects — the pressure has fallen on the consumer movement to keep the public informed about the dangers of these two addictive substances and to urge strict legislation to regulate their use.

Chapter Five

Transportation

When Ralph Nader's book *Unsafe at Any Speed* was published in 1965, the consumer movement was in its infancy. In many ways, Nader's book was the genesis of today's consumerism. It not only had a deep effect on the automotive industry, but it changed forever consumers' attitudes toward the products that they buy. In his book, Nader linked faulty engineering, inferior construction, and poor design to auto accidents and injuries. *Unsafe at Any Speed* captured the attention of the American public, and Nader became a household word as *the* consumer advocate.

In the same year, 1965, Senator Abraham Ribicoff convened a Senate committee to hold hearings on automobile safety. The committee hearings uncovered a shocking lack of concern on the part of auto industry executives for consumer safety. In a now-famous exchange, Senator Robert Kennedy, a member of the committee, was able to establish that General Motors had spent less than $2 million on its safety program; at the same time, its profits had totaled more than $1.5 billion.

With two developments — the publication of Nader's book and General Motors' unsuccessful attempt to discredit Nader — public concern mounted, which in turn placed pressure on the government. In 1966, the National Traffic and Motor Vehicle Safety Act was passed. This act authorized the establishment of the Highway Safety Administration (HSA), to be responsible for mandating compulsory safety standards for automobiles and tires. The HSA established guidelines for the recall of defective vehicles and, since its inception, has established more than thirty standards for automobiles, including dual braking systems and over-the-shoulder and interlocking seat belts in the front seat. Some new cars now have over-the-shoulder seat belts in the back seat as well.

Buckle Up for Safety

During the 1970's, seat-belt regulation was a focus of automobile safety. In an article titled "Buckle Up — Or Else," which appeared in *The Wall Street Journal* in 1973, before it was mandatory in many states to wear seat belts while driving — it was estimated that almost a third of the fifty thousand lives lost annually in automobile accidents could have been saved had the drivers been wearing their seat belts. Yet only about 20 percent of U.S. motorists were buckling up while traveling. By the 1980's, the federal government was offering incentives, such as highway funds, to induce states to pass seat-belt laws and enforce those laws.

Consumers' comparative lack of concern with safety issues has been attributed to a sense of optimism — that is, "It can happen to someone else, but is unlikely to happen to me." However, all the evidence points to the fact that accidents can happen to anyone, and using seat belts at all times during automobile travel has been proven to save many lives.

The consumer movement has used the volatile issue of auto safety to win much support from consumers who are generally apathetic. Naturally, car manufacturers have been resistant to meeting higher safety standards because of the high costs involved. A survey by Robert W. Crandall and associates, documented in their book *Regulating the Automobile* (1986), set out to determine whether the costs of more safety features for cars outweighed the advantages. The results showed that the benefits of increased auto safety did outweigh the costs. The two most significant automobile safety measures of the

U.S. Motor Vehicle Deaths per 100 Million Vehicle Miles

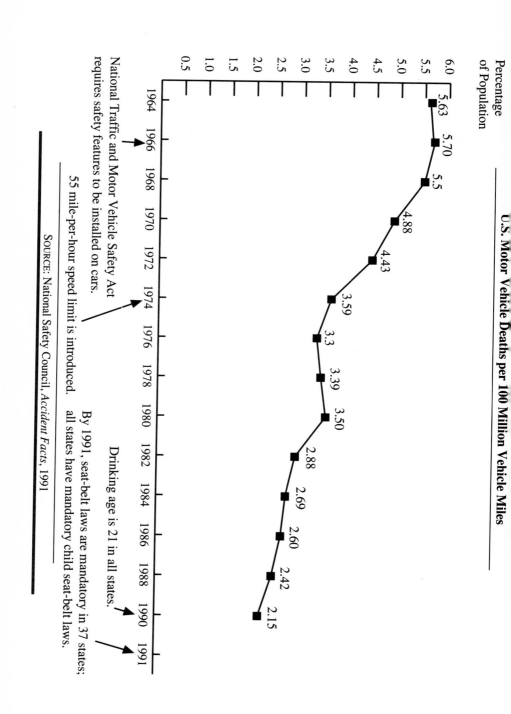

Percentage of Population

SOURCE: National Safety Council, *Accident Facts*, 1991

1980's — mandatory seat-belt use laws and child-restraint laws (car seats for children) — appear to be reaching their aim, which is to reduce both deaths and injuries on the road. In further efforts to decrease injuries and deaths in automobile accidents, the National Highway Traffic Safety Administration (NHTSA) has ruled on performance standards with regard to airbags. The Intermodal Surface Transportation Efficiency Act of 1991 requires airbags to be included in all cars and trucks by September 1, 1997.

The car manufacturer Volvo has led the way in auto safety, being the first with shoulder harnesses and among the first to equip its cars with airbags. Volvo has been a front-runner in environmentally safe automobiles as well: In the 1980's, Volvo was rated the least polluting vehicle (Saab was second) on a list kept by California's Air Resources Board.

Vehicle Recalls

Since Nader brought to public attention the disregard for safety on the part of the automobile manufacturers, there has been steady and effective pressure for government regulation to make roads and cars safer for travelers. After the National Traffic and Motor Vehicle Safety Act was passed in 1966, the Center for Auto Safety was founded in 1970 with an ambitious goal: to reduce the forty-six thousand motor vehicle deaths and the 1.7 million disabling injuries that occur annually in the United States.

The Center for Auto Safety has played a key role in many auto controversies. An example was the recall of 250,000 Audi 5000's. Several owners of these cars discovered a dangerous defect in the model's acceleration system which caused the car to "run away" unpredictably. The Center for Auto Safety was not satisfied with Audi's attempt to remedy the situation by installing a shift-lock device, so it urged the government to order Audi to repurchase the 5000 series.

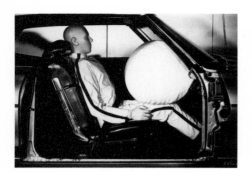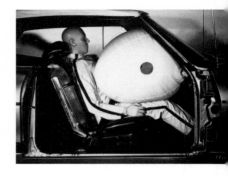
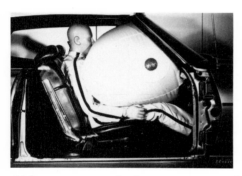

Airbags, now standard on some car models, can save lives in the event of a collision (National Highway Traffic Safety Administration)

Other automotive manufacturers in the United States have had to face recalls at one time or another due to violation of safety regulations. The Vega, a car unveiled by General Motors in 1971 as its answer to overseas rivals in the compact market, did not live up to expectations; it was costly and riddled with quality problems. In 1974, the Environmental Protection Agency (EPA) ordered the Chrysler Corporation to recall some 800,000 1973 light cars and trucks because of a defect in the exhaust gas recirculation system. In 1977, a record-number 10.7 million vehicles were recalled, the same amount of cars manufactured that year.

These are only a few examples of the recalls and malfunctions that have occurred over the years. The NHTSA views recalls on a case-by-case basis, so the Center for Auto Safety has no guarantee of success when lobbying; neither does this mean that the recall will eventually take place. However, as the Center for Auto Safety has demonstrated, sufficient pressure from consumer groups can force slow-moving government agencies to take action.

The Magnuson-Moss Warranty Act

Technological complexity tends to increase both production and repair problems in the manufacturing and use of products, whether those products are household appliances or automobiles. The modern American automobile, with some fourteen hundred parts, is much more complex than the first Model T Ford. Advances in technology during the twentieth century have brought great benefits, but also the risk of breakdowns and failures.

In 1975, Congress passed the Magnuson-Moss Warranty Act to ensure that the consumer is protected by warranty in the event of function failure. Under this act, a seller giving a "full" warranty is required to remedy the defective product within a reasonable time without charge to the buyer. In fact, the seller may be required to compensate a consumer for incidental expenses if the seller does not repair the product in a reasonable time.

Buying Used Cars

Nowhere has the consumer felt more powerless than when purchasing a vehicle, especially a used one. In some states, laws regulate the quality of used cars. Anyone who buys a used car from a reputable dealer can be assured that the car has been subjected to a safety inspection, which includes brakes, tires, lights, and steering. The key word, however, is "reputable": For example, the dealer may or may not change the timing belt at 60,000 miles, which is recommended by the manufacturer but not required by law before selling the car.

Anyone buying a used car from a dealer should get the 50-50 thirty-day "power train" warranty. This warranty covers the purchaser for 50 percent of the costs of both parts and labor for repairs needed within thirty days of purchase. The power train normally covers only those repairs done at the dealership. The dealer usually advises the consumer to purchase an extended warranty plan. In many instances, the purchase of such an extended plan may be advisable, but it pays to read all the fine print. For example, does the dealer's warranty stipulate that the car must be repaired by that dealer? If so, it pays to have a dealership that is both trustworthy and situated in a convenient, nearby location.

Buying New Cars: Lemon Laws

First enacted in Connecticut in 1980, lemon laws are designed to help consumers when a new car has serious defects that cannot be easily repaired. A typical lemon law states that a consumer is entitled to a refund or a new car if a serious defect has not been corrected in four attempts or if the car has been out of commission for repairs for a total of thirty days or more under the original warranty. In practice, a person dissatisfied with a new car may still have to bring a private legal action to enforce lemon laws.

If consumers have any complaints about vehicle repairs or warranties, they should return to the dealer with the complaint. In a dispute, the consumer should present all documentation, including receipts and warranties, to the car dealer or repair shop. If the dealer or repair shop is unresponsive, the consumer can generally appeal to a state agency that oversees such matters. In California, this agency is the Bureau of Automotive Repairs, which deals with consumers' complaints about repairs. The consumer should also consult the Council of Better Business Bureaus' Auto Hotline Program. (Check Robert Wilson's *Consumer Sourcebook*, listed in "Publications" at the end of this volume, for state-by-state phone numbers of these groups.)

Stickers posted on the windows of new cars reveal basic information about the car's features and cost. (Tony Freeman/PhotoBank)

Energy Consumption and Conservation

The Energy Policy and Conservation Act of 1975 imposed corporate average fuel economy (CAFE) standards on car manufacturers. The standards began at 18 miles per gallon (mpg) and gradually increased to 27.5 for the 1985 model year. The act also requires that manufacturers place mpg stickers on cars so that consumers can compare the fuel efficiency of vehicles before making a decision on which car to purchase.

In practice, however, CAFE has done little to reduce energy consumption. Instead, the effect has been to force American automobile manufacturers to face stiffer competition from Japan's fuel-efficient cars, particularly after trade restrictions with Japan were lifted during the early years of the Reagan Administration. American car manufacturers had made a serious mistake in thinking that Americans would not buy Japanese cars. In 1986, responding to pressure from Ford and General Motors, the Department of Transportation lowered CAFE standards.

These issues highlight how complex consumer interests are, and how consumer interest groups may even conflict with one another. Conserving the earth's resources, for example, is important to all consumers, but it is to the advantage of car manufacturers (who provide jobs for workers and cars for consumers) to work under fewer restrictions. Ideally, both interests can be served if car manufacturers produce more fuel-efficient cars.

Nader Takes On the Airlines

After World War II ended, more and more people began to travel by airplane. The greater demand for this form of transportation resulted from a growing birth rate and higher incomes, which in turn contributed to a more mobile population. Today, business travelers will frequently take day trips between one state and another, or between major cities.

In 1972, Allegheny Airlines refused to let Ralph Nader board one of its planes, saying that the plane was full, even though he had a ticket. At that time, customers holding confirmed bookings had no recourse should they arrive at the gate and find the plane filled. When Nader filed a lawsuit, he not only sought redress for discrimination against him but also sought to bring about a new ruling that would ban overbooking by airlines. According to some analysts, this 1973 ruling by the Civil Aeronautics Board, which prohibited airlines from overbooking flights, favored passengers over airlines, which now lost money as they could no longer overbook. However, the rule on overbooking has been weakened since deregulation in 1978.

Airline Deregulation

Since 1958, the airline industry has been regulated for safety by the Federal Aviation Administration (FAA). The Civil Aeronautics Board (CAB) controlled the industry for economic purposes. In 1978, Congress formally began economic deregulation of the airlines with the passage of the Airline Deregulation Act.

During the Reagan Administration, there was further deregulation of airlines, and in 1985 the CAB was dismantled and its remaining responsibilities were transferred to the Department of Transportation. The airline industry was riddled with problems, some of which came from a strike by members of the air traffic controllers' union. Part of the reason for deregulation was to bring about more competitive air fares for the consumer and more profits for the airline carrier, but that did not come to pass. Although some studies have shown increased competition with more airline carriers, airlines have not seen higher profits and, in fact, have in several cases (notably that of Pan Am) have become extinct in the face of skyrocketing costs.

Studies done on the effects of deregulation have shown that in general prices to consumers have remained stable, but some analysts believe that deregulation has compromised safety for passengers as airlines cut corners on maintaining aging equipment in order to reduce operating costs. This concern has been fueled by an upsurge of airline accidents and near-collisions, despite studies done in the early 1980's that showed an improvement in safety after deregulation. More studies need to be done to establish whether traveling by airplane is now safer or less safe than before. Whatever conclusions are drawn, consumers have a right to airline safety. It is the task of consumer activists to continue to monitor whether the FAA is fulfilling is mandate: to regulate and ensure safety for airline passengers.

As Americans generate more income and often have to travel farther to reach better-paying jobs, transportation has become a priority of government regulating agencies and consumer activists. This has made consumers dependent on protective agencies regulating the automobile industry, such as the NHTSA, and the FAA, which regulates safety in the airline industry. However, the 1980's were notable for cutbacks in federal spending and a movement toward deregulation, which has weakened federal controls over private companies and undermined the enforcement of existing regulations.

Chapter Six

Toys
and
Appliances

A typical American family home has a wide range of appliances, household equipment, and children's toys. All these items can pose a serious safety risk unless they have been thoroughly tested and approved for consumers' use. Sellers, of course, claim that much of the product injury problem is caused by the environment or improper use by the owner. Consumer advocates, on the other hand, claim that product design is the primary factor in product-related injuries.

When purchasing children's toys, consumers should consider safety first and price second. Parents must also be aware that older children are able to buy toys on their own, without parental supervision. This places them at risk, particularly because children are unlikely to read warning labels.

Children can abuse toys in a way that it is difficult for parents or other caretakers to envisage. This places the burden on the seller to put the toy through rigorous and punishing testing to establish whether the toy can withstand a child's usage. Some of the marketing problems that toy manufacturers have encountered have been caused by their reluctance to take these factors into account. There are still stuffed animals available whose eyes can be easily pulled off, or which shed significant amounts of fur when cuddled; both these factors are dangerous for young children.

During congressional hearings on toy safety in 1969, a toy oven was presented for consideration. The oven, when turned on, was too hot to touch, with an inside temperature of 600 degrees Fahrenheit. This "toy" definitely posed an unreasonable hazard for young children.

Although it is every parent's responsibility to protect his or her child, it is unreasonable to expect parents to be responsible for the safe design and honest marketing of toys. It is the manufacturer, not the parent, who has the control over a toy's design. It is up to the manufacturer, therefore, to make sure that toys are safe, and for government agencies to act on consumer complaints.

- Wear a helmet, elbow pads, knee pads, and gloves.
- Learn to stop safely.
- Skate on smooth, paved surfaces without any traffic.
- Avoid skating at night.

In-line roller skates can be extremely dangerous; adults should monitor the use of these "toys." (Consumer Product Safety Commission)

The Child Protection and Toy Safety Act

After congressional hearings, the Child Protection and Toy Safety Act was passed in 1969. The Child Protection Act of 1966 had banned from the market all toys or other articles that bore or contained hazardous substances and were intended for use by children. The Child Protection and Toy Safety Act of 1969 broadened the protection by banning any toys that constituted mechanical, electrical, or fire hazards. (Some toys were exempt — for example, chemistry sets, which contain potentially hazardous substances but are designed to be used by older children.)

The Child Protection and Toy Safety Act has done much to protect children and has forced toy manufacturers to place more emphasis on issuing legible warnings and proper instructions with toys. However, it would be unwise for parents to take for granted that this law can keep all unsafe toys off the market. The example of stuffed animal toys noted above is a case in point. Swap meets and 99-cent stores are some of the places where toys that do not meet current standards may still be bought. Another factor is that products enter and leave the toy market at a much higher rate than conventional products. An unsafe toy can be available on the market and can be sold in quantities before it comes to the attention of regulatory authorities.

The Federal Drug Administration (FDA) announced in June, 1972, that more than 200,000 toys had been recalled in the past six months. These included squeeze dolls, rattles, musical balls, and wooden soldiers. In 1973, the responsibility for toy safety was transferred from the FDA, which had few resources to act against unsafe toys, to the newly created Consumer Product Safety Commission in an effort to monitor toys on the market more effectively. One major recall by the Consumer Product Safety Commission was of five million Mattel Battlestar Galactica toy missiles for faulty construction, which posed a health hazard. Still, there has been little regulatory activity with regard to toys since the 1969 act.

Child-Resistant Closures

Children not only like to play with toys; they also like to remove the tops of bottles and jars, such as those in the medicine cabinet. In 1970, Congress passed the Poison Prevention Packaging Act. The goal was to protect children from dangerous substances found in homes — such as aspirin, prescription drugs, drain cleaner, paint thinner, and furniture polish.

Unfortunately, a follow-up study did not indicate any decrease in accidents involving children four years and younger due to ingesting poisonous substances. One of the reasons cited for this apparent lack of effect was that, because child-resistant caps are so hard to open, some parents leave the tops off the bottles for their own convenience. Another reason given was that some parents may become complacent, thinking a "child-proof" container is safe, and therefore leave it within the reach of their children.

In his book *Regulating Consumer Safety* (1984), Kip Viscusi criticizes the overall performance of the Consumer Product Safety Commission. He bases his criticism on research which revealed that regulating a product does not necessarily increase consumers' safety, if a related product is not also regulated. For example, by 1972 aspirin had child-resistant caps, but a leading brand of acetaminophen was not regulated until 1980. There was a decline of accidental deaths related to aspirin, but at the same time there was an increase in accidental deaths related to the analgesic containing acetaminophen. Viscusi charges that consumers were lulled into carelessness with the acetaminophen product because they were treating it as they would treat the aspirin products.

Equipment and Appliances

Equipment and furniture, such as cribs, have also been regulated as a result of faulty construction that has caused injury and even death. Between 1970 and 1973, the FDA received death certificates for 133 children whose deaths were related to problems in the structure of their cribs. By late 1973, the Consumer Product Safety Commission had imposed standards, such as a minimum distance between slats in cribs, intended to make child-related equipment safer. According to the Commission's report in 1979, crib-related injuries had declined by 44 percent and deaths by 33 percent after the new standard was imposed.

Other equipment in the home that has been regulated to provide greater safety includes mattresses and hair dryers, which are now less flammable because they are free of asbestos. An example of a recall as a result of safety violations was the Department of Housing and Urban Development's removal of some two thousand Tappan gas stoves from mobile homes because of gas leaks and the threat of explosions. Sears-Roebuck recalled six thousand gas heaters after being notified of potentially fatal leakages.

Microwave ovens have caused a revolution in many households, making the preparation of food both faster and more convenient. However, their safety has been questioned. In April, 1973, the FDA ruled that all microwave ovens be equipped with back-up switch-off devices, to guard against radiation exposure should the primary switch-off device fail. The month before this ruling, the Consumers Union had reported that fifteen leading microwave oven models had shown "measurable radiation leakage." In 1975, the FDA issued a warning about possible radiation damage from some twelve thousand General Electric microwave ovens and urged owners to have the ovens inspected before further use.

Despite regulations, Americans are still injured or killed each year as a result of faulty equipment in the home. There are three elements that the legal system considers in any product-related injury: the environmental conditions at the time of injury, the condition of the user of the product, and the product itself. To illustrate, consider the case of a man who cuts his lawn after a day at the office just before it gets dark. While he is cutting his grass, the mower hits a stone, which flies up in the air and injures his son. The product may be at fault, lacking a shield to deflect projectiles such as rocks. However, other factors may be involved. The man may have been tired and may not have taken the precaution of clearing the area before mowing; perhaps he was mowing the lawn at dusk, and there was not enough light to allow him to see where he was going.

With some products, however, the cause is very clear. In 1968, the National Commission on Product Safety investigated floor gas furnaces that reached very high, even hazardous, temperatures. By the time the Commission convened in 1968, these furnaces were the leading cause of burns in children under five years old and accounted for one in five burns in children up to the age of fifteen.

In cases where the cause of an injury is not clearly defined, a product's design may determine the severity of the injury if not actually cause the injury. Consumers may not consider this fact when suffering an injury from a product. A 1978 landmark case in California, *Barker v. Lull Engineering Co.*, shifted the burden of proof in design defects from the consumer to the manufacturer. It was ruled that the manufacturer must show that the usefulness of a product outweighs the risks intrinsic in its design.

What Consumers Say

What do the surveys show when measuring consumer satisfaction? A 1972 survey conducted by General Electric asked forty-eight thousand respondents to comment on their overall satisfaction or dissatisfaction with some 665,000 individual appliances.

There was a high satisfaction rate, 94 percent, at the time of the survey. Sears did a comparable survey with similar results. A 1975 survey, sponsored by two consumer action groups, found much more discouraging results. In this survey, about 28 percent of all purchases were found to be unsatisfactory in some respect. Many of the complaints were price-related, and high on the list were complaints about lack of service and faulty repairs. In the middle range were complaints about household appliances and televisions. The wide differences in the results of such surveys suggest how limited they may be. Also, most dissatisfied consumers do not respond to surveys.

In general, consumers do not voice problems to either retailers or manufacturers. Consumer complaints that have been made to the FTC have involved delays in repairs, faultily designed products, excessive labor charges, failure of the retailer or service organization to honor the guarantee, and lack of form for redress. For change to take place, it is crucial for consumers to make complaints to the appropriate agency and to write to their representative in Congress with suggestions for how to improve warranties on products and protect consumers from inadequate service and repair.

Warnings and Warranties

Consumers can also protect themselves by reading all instructions and warnings on a product before using it, and by filling out manufacturers' warranties at the time of purchase. It was due to problems in warranties that the Magnuson-Moss Warranty Act was passed in 1975 in order to reform consumer product warranty practices. Under this act, a seller giving a "full" warranty is required to remedy the defective product within a reasonable time without charge. In fact, the seller may be required to compensate a consumer for incidental expenses should the seller not repair the product within a reasonable time.

A basic cause of warranty problems has been that consumers and warrantors have quite different perceptions of the role that a warranty plays in the marketplace. For the consumer, the mere existence of a warranty is a positive influence when he or she purchases a product. However, a warranty may not reflect product quality but be a marketing device to lure customers. Under the Uniform Commercial Code — which is in effect in all U.S. states except Louisiana — most sales of goods are covered by an "implied" warranty even if an "actual" warranty does not exist. In other words, the product is *warranted* as being able to do what it is designed to do, and the consumer is protected by that assurance at the time of purchase and for a limited time thereafter (such as ninety days), depending on the nature of the breakdown and usage.

What happens when a consumer complains to the retailer or manufacturer and does not receive a satisfactory response? The consumer can then approach the Federal Trade Commission or a consumers' protection body. The latest edition of *Consumer Sourcebook* lists organizations that people can contact when redress is not available through the retailer or manufacturer; it also lists places to contact to learn how to file complaints.

Chapter Seven

Services and Mail-Order Goods

Services make up a significant portion of the economy. Consumers are increasingly involved in transactions with those who provide services: banks and credit companies, car and health insurance providers, contractors who build and repair homes, and attorneys, to name a few.

Banking Deregulation

The consumer movement has directly affected a number of important laws and regulations governing the banking industry. The 1968 Truth-in-Lending Act required banks and lending organizations to give full disclosure of their credit terms. This meant that a customer would be able to know exactly his or her monthly payments, whether there would be any large "balloon" payment at the end of the payment period, and, if so, how much.

In the early 1980's, several acts brought about fundamental changes in banking. Regulations that controlled interest rates and charges for banking services were largely eliminated. In

1987, Congress passed legislation limiting the period during which a bank can hold a check before crediting it to the customer's account. Previously, the bank could determine how long it would hold the check. Currently, a bank can hold a local check for up to two days, and an out-of-state check for up to five days. With the deregulation of bank charges, many banks penalized smaller accounts with higher rates. This has adversely affected the poor and the elderly, but consumerists pressured banks to initiate programs to provide for these groups. Many consumers took advantage of the new ruling and were able to switch from checking accounts that earned no interest to checking accounts that did; altogether, these interest-bearing accounts yielded consumers more than $10 billion in 1986.

The most far-reaching consequence of banking deregulation (that is, the reduction of controls over how a business operates) has been the controversy over savings and loan institutions (S&Ls). Deregulation allowed banks and S&Ls to offer loans with less security than previously. The late 1980's witnessed the drop in oil prices and an unstable economy, which resulted in many borrowers with large debts defaulting on their loans. This, in turn, triggered the collapse of a number of S&Ls, as well as banks. What compounded the problem is that S&Ls had acted irresponsibly with investors' money by making very risky investments with that money. Investments in "junk bonds," for example, promised high returns but were very uncertain. The Federal Deposit Insurance Corporation (FDIC) protects every investor for up to $100,000. Therefore, the savings and loan fiasco not only depleted FDIC reserves but also forced the federal government to become involved in protecting major investors and preventing a massive collapse of the savings and loan system. Unfortunately, it is the taxpayers — for the most part, uninvolved consumers — who will spend years paying the bill.

Consumers who use credit pay the price: Credit card companies charge extra money, or "interest," each time we buy on credit. (Paul Conklin/Uniphoto)

Credit Cards and Credit Reporting

Countless consumers have found themselves in financial trouble due to overspending on credit cards. Using a credit card to shop by mail and telephone has made it easier to accumulate debt, as well as rendering consumers vulnerable to credit card fraud. A 1970 ruling protected consumers from credit card fraud by limiting their liability to $50 for stolen cards used without authorization. Previously it was up to consumers to buy credit card protection. If a seller wrongfully bills a consumer on his or her credit card, it is still up to the consumer to settle the dispute with the seller.

The interest rates on credit cards are some of the highest on the market. Consumers are advised to compare interest rates and shop around for lower card fees per year. Paying off a credit card by the end of the month is the surest way to eliminate interest charges.

One area of consumer concern has to do with the practice of credit reporting. Large corporations, including TRW, Equifax, and Transunion, keep records on holders of credit cards, tracking their expenditures, payments, and outstanding debts. If a consumer defaults on a payment or fails to pay altogether, that information is placed in the consumer's file and is available to any seller from whom the consumer may wish to purchase goods on credit. Occasionally, consumers have discovered that errors have appeared in their credit reports: old debts have not been removed, or the debts of one person have been mistakenly assigned to another person with the same name. Such errors can be devastating to an innocent person, causing hardship for years.

Because of rising consumer complaints about errors on their credit reports, the Federal Trade Commission (FTC) requires credit reporting companies to monitor the accuracy of their files on a regular basis. By the end of 1991, Congress was considering changes to the Fair Credit Reporting Act of 1970. Until that time, consumers had to pay credit reporting companies a fee in order to obtain information in their files (unless they had been denied credit, in which case they could obtain such a report free of charge within a limited period of time). In January, 1992, one company, TRW, announced that consumers would be able to receive one free copy of their credit report each year.

The Price of Insurance

In the last quarter of the twentieth century, insurance costs have skyrocketed. Auto insurance rates have risen significantly, particularly in large metropolitan areas, where crime has also increased. A proposition passed in California in 1990 was insufficient to keep the lid on auto insurance rates, which in many cases is so unaffordable that more and more drivers are breaking the law by driving without insurance.

Perhaps even more serious is the increasing cost of health care, and consequently of medical insurance. During the decade of the 1980's, medical insurance rates rose approximately 200 percent. Consumers who do not have full coverage through their employers have to take on insurance with higher deductibles (that is, they must pay a larger sum before coverage will take effect). While this may protect them from the big bills such as hospital costs, it can still mean hardship for a family who has to come up with $500 or more for some standard tests or to X-ray and set a broken limb. Many people in the medical field, as well as economists and politicians, believe that the health-care system in the United States is in crisis, and that the availability of good medical care is in a severe decline.

Especially hard hit are the elderly and others who have "pre-existing conditions" that disqualify them for affordable insurance. "Pre-existing" refers to chronic, or ongoing, illness that started before coverage with the insurance company began. Insurers often will not cover the cost of care related to such long-term illnesses. An elderly person with cancer, for example, is usually not able to get sufficient care through Medicare and, because cancer is often considered a pre-existing condition, may not be able to find supplemental coverage. Those with the HIV virus or full-blown AIDS either cannot get health insurance or, if it is available, cannot afford the extremely high premiums. They often must rely on home nursing and hospices during the terminal stages of their illness. In an innovative move, several life insurance companies have allowed clients suffering from AIDS to cash in their life insurance in order to pay for medical costs.

For complaints about insurance, consumers are primarily represented by the National Insurance Consumer Organization (NICO). NICO was originally established to help consumers buy insurance wisely and to eliminate abusive practices by the insurance industry. In recent years, however, NICO has concentrated on commercial liability insurance. Consumers are advised to contact their state insurance commissioner if they have a complaint. This office helps consumers with personal insurance problems unresolved by their own insurance companies and assists consumers in the purchase of insurance policies. The Consumer Insurance Interest Group is an independent consumer advocacy group that works cooperatively with the insurance industry. Their publications include *Consumer Watch: Tips on Insurance*. Another group that serves consumers is the Health Insurance Association of America, which works to reduce health-care costs and monitors the quality of and access to health services.

Mail-Order Shopping

High on consumers' list of complaints has been mail-order shopping. Ordering through a catalog is a little like buying a product sight-unseen. At best, photographs and written descriptions are poor substitutions for firsthand inspection. At worst, a product may appear to be better than it is, and essential information about it may not be provided. Even if a mail-order outlet has a flexible returns policy, no consumer wants the inconvenience of mailing back a defective product. Some unscrupulous mail-order companies may hope that consumers who buy their low-quality products will not bother to complain or return them.

Some credit card companies offer shopping by mail with the added incentive of using their card to earn "points" toward purchases in their catalogue. Consumers should beware of the prices of these products; often they cost the same or more than they would cost through a discount outlet that will even take that credit card.

To protect consumers, the FTC has ruled, in its Mail-Order Merchandising Rule, that a seller must ship an order within

U.S. taxpayers — consumers — will spend millions of dollars to "bail out" savings and loan institutions. (Uniphoto)

thirty days of receiving the order. Failure to do so gives the buyer the right to cancel the order and receive a full refund. Consumers who have received defective goods through the mail and have not received satisfaction from the mail-order company should contact the Federal Trade Commission's Bureau of Consumer Protection.

Fraud and the Class Action Suit

One of the traditional concerns of the consumer movement has been the campaign against fraud. The combined efforts of Ralph Nader and the American Bar Association revitalized the Federal Trade Commission's ability to tackle this problem. Virtually every state now has a consumer fraud bureau in the office of the attorney general; many of these offices have legal power exceeding that of the FTC.

However, many businesses committing fraud are in business for only a few years, which makes it difficult if not impossible for the FTC to track them down. Unfortunately, serious consumer fraud continues to be committed daily in metropolitan areas. The hardest hit are the poor, who often are too afraid or lack the knowledge to follow through with complaints.

As a rule of thumb, consumers should always avoid paying for goods before they receive them, even if the company with which they are dealing is well known and reputable. One way to check is through a local Better Business Bureau; however, these agencies are often besieged by queries and lack the resources to be on top of every fraudulent business. For example, since the late 1970's, pyramid sales schemes have flourished. Most small pyramid sales schemes do not deliver what they promise, and investors will find themselves losing their investments.

One way consumers can become empowered is through the class action suit. This is a suit in which one person sues to recover damages not only for himself or herself but also for other persons similarly involved. In a class action suit a group of consumers can seek compensation as a single party; this way they have more economic resources in filing the suit than if they did it alone. The United States is an innovator of class action suits; even antitrust violations such as price fixing can be challenged by class action suits.

If a consumer wins a class action suit, all other consumers who were injured by the same company get their money back too, even though they did not personally participate in the lawsuit. For example, in Illinois, Montgomery Ward was found to have charged its credit customers wrongfully for credit life insurance whether they asked for it or not. A class action forced the firm to pay some $5,700,000 to 110,000 customers.

Like the lemon laws for automobiles, however, class action suits are more impressive in principle than in practice. To bring a federal class action suit in the United States, a consumer must show that neither individual legal action nor joint suits by small groups who allegedly were harmed by the same product or service is practicable. The harm must be similar for the whole group, not a situation in which some members were affected in some way and others in another way. Further, class action suits can also be expensive: Legal fees can eat up a third or more of the damages paid to consumers if they win.

Despite these disadvantages, a class action suit can still help consumers. Most important of all, it can make fraudulent service providers think twice about taking advantage of the public.

Chapter Eight

The Environment

The growth of technology and industrialization, along with significant population increases, has come at a price: an environment in jeopardy. What was uppermost in consumer activists' minds at the beginning of the twentieth century was the quality of food and the safety of drugs. By the twenty-first century, the environment — specifically, how to deal with toxic wastes and how to assure clean, oxygenated air and water that can support life — will be at the forefront of consumerism.

The modern environmental movement emerged in the 1960's, but in part was a return to the activism of older conservation groups in America that had fought to preserve the country's natural resources. Today, environmental consumerists can be divided into two groups. A group of consumerists that can be called *radical consumers* is opposed to new technologies until they are proven "innocent." Radicals fear that the U.S. consumer, who is usually "economically driven" (that is, motivated by cost and other economic concerns), will vote in favor of technology that is cost-effective, at the expense of the environment. Radicals, for example, have opposed the use of nuclear power as an energy source, citing it as potentially hazardous. Nuclear disasters such as those at Three Mile Island in 1979 and at the Soviet Union's Chernobyl nuclear power plant in 1986 have confirmed radicals' fears of nuclear danger. Ralph Nader, a longtime critic of nuclear energy, is in the forefront of radical consumers: His Critical Mass organization is one of the major antinuclear groups.

Radical consumerists are also concerned that the hazards to the environment posed by runaway technology will reach crisis proportions by the second quarter of the twenty-first century, at which point, they believe, the world will have to deal with an overflow of toxic and carcinogenic substances.

Another group of consumerists, *reformist consumers*, take a different attitude: They view technology as neither bad nor good, but something that is open to good use or abuse. For example, reformists will criticize the use of aerosol sprays, which emit chlorofluorocarbons (CFCs) that have damaged the atmosphere's protective ozone layer. At the same time, reformists will embrace technology such as airbags, smoke detectors, and solar power. To this extent, reformists and radicals would agree. Reformists, however, would consider nuclear power as a clean, cost-effective alternative to oil-based energy, whereas radicals reject both as dangerous.

Litter is not only ugly to look at, but also it is dangerous to the environment. (Environmental Protection Agency)

Consumerism vs. Environmentalism

The consumer movement is made up of *primary activists*, such as those lobbying for auto safety and formal avenues for consumer redress on faulty goods, and of *secondary consumerists*, with whom they might sometimes, but not always, form alliances. One such group of secondary consumerists is the environmentalists.

Sometimes consumer activists are in conflict with environmentalists, who may believe that consumerists are willing to "sell out" the environment for lower prices or greater consumer convenience. For example, the widely read magazine *Consumer Reports* will rate different brands of disposable diapers; environmentalists would prefer that *Consumer Reports* reject disposable diapers entirely, in favor of more environmentally sound (reusable) cloth ones. Yet, manufacturers of disposable diapers are responding to the current trend (and pressure) toward more ecologically sound products; they are developing diapers that are more easily biodegradable.

In Europe, environmentalists have gained political ground with the increased representation of the Green party in governments. In 1992, the Green party gained a small, but significant, foothold in the United States by qualifying for the ballot in a few states. The rise in the prominence of this group has accompanied growing public awareness of the shrinking South American rain forests and the impact of their loss on air quality.

Other environmental groups that have enough clout to bring about changes in laws are the National Wildlife Federation, the National Audubon Society, the Sierra Club, and the Natural Resources Defense Council. Greenpeace and Earth First! are more radical groups committed to preserving all life on the planet; they sometimes take dramatic steps to get a point across. For example, Greenpeace has thrown its tiny boats in the path of whaling ships in order to stop whaling. This organization has also positioned its boats in the South Pacific, under the protection of New Zealand, a declared nuclear-free zone, to protest and prevent nuclear testing. In 1970, after the first "Earth Day" mobilized thousands of Americans, the word "ecology" suddenly entered the American vocabulary. Environmental organizations were formed — such as the Environmental Defense Fund, Friends of the Earth, and Environmental Action.

Getting the Lead Out

The hazards of lead in the environment have been known for some time. In the 1970's, legislation was passed banning lead-based paints. People are still being subjected to lead-based paint, however, if they live in older buildings that have not yet been repainted. These buildings pose a hazard because the paint is now old and peeling; babies, who tend to put everything in their mouths, are particularly at risk for lead poisoning, which can cause irreversible brain retardation in infants and children.

Lead also became a peril through its presence in leaded gasoline. It was finally regulated in the 1970's. The United States was far ahead of Europe in introducing unleaded gasoline to control lead emissions. It was only in the mid-1980's that unleaded gasoline was available in England. Despite initial reluctance on the part of manufacturers and consumers — including complaints that cars did not run as well with the lower-octane gasoline — unleaded gasoline is now accepted as a necessity in an increasingly compromised environment.

Protecting Rivers and Lakes

Manufacturers have been responding to the pressure from the EPA to produce more environmentally conscious products in the effort to reduce pollution of rivers and lakes. One way that soap manufacturers have responded is by reducing polluting phosphates in their products. Sears, for example, introduced a phosphate-free detergent in the late 1970's, and other washing-powder manufacturers have followed suit. Other major sources of pollution in rivers and lakes include by-products generated by the manufacturing industry. Another environmental problem generated by industrial growth is "acid rain." This is a term given to rain that has mixed with chemical pollutants in the air, forming acidic compounds. When it rains, these compounds are introduced into groundwater and may eventually make their way into human drinking water.

The 1990 Clean Air Act Amendments

The Clean Air Act Amendments of 1990, signed by President George Bush in November, signified a new era in environmental regulation. The amendments promise to offer solutions to some of the most resistant environmental problems. Among other things, the amendments will within the first two years of enactment:

(1)   remove 56 billion pounds a year of pollution from the air;
(2)   reduce by 50 percent emissions causing acid rain; and
(3)   reduce by 75 percent emissions resulting from toxic air pollutants.

These goals will be achieved, according to the amendments, because the EPA will work closely with its regional offices to monitor more stringently businesses and industries that generate pollution. The aim is to take a tougher stance against those companies that violate existing regulations on air quality control.

Consumer groups have also focused on reducing car

We are choking in our own car exhaust. (Environmental Protection Agency)

emissions in such metropolitan areas as Los Angeles, a city besieged by smog and cars due to an inadequate public transport system. In Southern California, smog tests have to be done on cars every other year. Cars must pass these emissions tests or be repaired before owners can have their registrations renewed. This law resulted from a combination of consumer action and recommendations of the California Air Quality Management Board.

The Vanishing Ozone

In the early 1980's, the average consumer was not familiar with the term "global warming." This term refers to a process that is occurring in the earth's atmosphere called the "greenhouse effect": With increased air pollution, more carbon dioxide, and less oxygen, is in the atmosphere. As a result, more of the sun's heat becomes "trapped" inside the earth's atmospheric layer, just as heat becomes trapped on a hot day inside a car with its windows rolled up. Also, earth's "ozone layer," which has protected it from the sun's hot rays, has been deteriorating because of air pollution. As more scientific data emerge about how the ozone layer is becoming depleted and the consequent dangers of ultraviolet radiation from the sun, such as increased melanoma (a deadly form of skin cancer), there is an added burden on consumers to be environmentally responsible in the choice of products.

The chief culprit in ozone loss is the presence of *chlorofluorocarbons* (CFCs). This is not easy to fix, because CFCs are used in many common substances and devices: in aerosols, in refrigerators and air conditioners, in cleaning solvents in factories, and as blowing agents to create certain kinds of plastic foam. Manufacturers are becoming more sensitive to protecting the ozone layer, and one way they can do this is to eliminate aerosol sprays. When an aerosol can is used, CFCs escape into the atmosphere and eventually make their way to the ozone layer, where they destroy the chemical balance that produces the protective ozone. Scientists have been amazed at how rapidly this deterioration has occurred in recent years. Many aerosol-spray deodorants, hair products, and household cleaners are being replaced by pump-spray products. Technology is also being developed to find substitutes for CFCs and to recycle CFCs from refrigerators.

Ecological Marketing

Ecological marketing is a strategy to remedy the environmental crisis. Here, the U.S. government has played the role of educator rather than regulator. Instead of focusing on providing consumers with products, the goal is to decrease consumers' demands for products that are not compatible with a cleaner environment.

Environmentally safe products are ones that protect the earth from pollutants and preserve natural resources. These products include goods packed in recyclable materials such as paper rather than plastics; reusable cloth shopping bags, which save paper and therefore trees; and phosphate-free, biodegradable soaps, which do not contaminate groundwater or kill fish. (A "biodegradable" substance is one that will break down into chemical components that the earth can absorb without harm to plants or animals, including humans.)

Ecologically aware manufacturers have to entice consumers away from the giant manufacturers. In the past, "environmentally conscious" products have not been able to compete with the sophisticated design and packaging of mainstream products, but that is changing: Ecologically aware manufacturers are designing attractive packages that compete with other products. The end of the century will likely see a host of stores and centers that carry environmentally conscious products, such as the Seed Center in Santa Fe, New Mexico. The Seed Center is a place where people can browse, talk to environmental experts, buy safe products, or use computers that are part of an environmental information network.

Recycling: Resources for the Future

In 1975, 90 percent of a nationwide cross section of adults in the United States indicated that they would be willing to cut down on the plastic bags and packages they were accustomed to getting with the goods they bought. Yet, throwaway packaging is very much part of the convenience that consumers increasingly want in a technological society. In 1973, consumers and commercial firms generated waste of 144 million tons, as noted by the Environmental Protection Agency.

Recycling was a fringe phenomenon in the 1970's and gathered momentum in the 1980's. Recycling does not reduce the level of waste, but it is an ecologically desirable way to handle waste. Today, recycling is a necessity, not an option: Landfills are running out, and people will soon drown in their

*Recycling and making less trash—**less** consumption—are only the first steps toward restoring the environment.* (Susan Hormuth)

own trash if they do nothing. Newspapers are now printed on predominantly recycled paper; plastic, glass, and aluminum containers are routinely recycled; and many packaged and paper goods display the recycle logo. More and more neighborhoods, businesses, and apartment and condominium complexes have recycling plans, sometimes by arrangement with a waste management firm. "Recycling centers" can be found at convenient locations, such as supermarkets; these facilities have bins where paper, glass, and plastic can be left. In addition, many cities are beginning to pick up and recycle sorted trash left on the curb on special days of the week.

As the population grows, so does the trash that people produce. In the 1970's, ecologically conscious consumers ranged between 20 and 30 percent of the population. It was estimated that those figures had risen by 10 percent by the late 1980's. By 1991, a compromised economy had brought about a downturn in American consumer attitudes — just as two landmark pieces of environmental legislation, the Endangered Species Act and the Clean Water Act, were up for renewal in Congress. Jobs became more important than saving trees, and environmentalists faced stiff opposition from anti-green advocates such as developers and manufacturers. Until the economy improves or the priorities of society change, the outlook for environmentalism is uncertain. Consumers hold the key to the solution of the waste problem.

Chapter Nine

The Future of Consumerism

Even as the consumer movement was growing and maturing in the 1960's, many predicted that consumer activism, or consumerism, would wane and eventually die out. Yet, the consumer movement has been instrumental in the passage of many important laws that have enhanced the quality of life for consumers. Despite the lull in the late 1970's and 1980's, the consumer movement continues to be active and faces new challenges from increased technology, an emerging global economy, and a depressed world economy.

The Growth of Imported Goods

Any change in production, distribution, and consumption of goods will raise consumer issues in the future. For example, today many goods sold in North America and Western Europe have been produced abroad; some of these goods are produced in developing nations. Because standards of product safety and performance vary from nation to nation, products may be imported into the United States that fall below American standards. With the increased flow of imported goods, more counterfeit goods slip through. These goods are often inferior to the goods they imitate.

Another issue of imported goods is the question of who takes responsibility for defective goods. For example, a bicycle importer sold a retailer fifty imported bicycles, which were later suspected of safety violations, although no accident occurred. When the retailer approached the importer about this, the importer refused to take responsibility. The manufacturer was halfway across the world and very difficult to reach. Fortunately, the retailer decided to take the responsibility and recalled all fifty bicycles and found a way to absorb the costs.

Consumers are also concerned over whether there should be more laws protecting domestically produced goods. In 1983, for example, Americans paid $71 billion in higher prices as a result of trade restrictions on imported goods. Domestic manufacturers benefitted, but the consumer did not. Although such protections can benefit the domestic economy, and in that sense the consumer, these trade restrictions can also "protect" manufacturers from competing with foreign goods that may be superior in quality.

Food for Thought

Consumers are growing more worried about the food they eat. In 1987, salmonella outbreaks were directly related to poultry processing techniques. At least one consumer group, the Community Nutrition Institute, urged consumers to boycott poultry until the Department of Agriculture took steps to safeguard the poultry supply. The choice was difficult for consumers, because in rejecting poultry they may equally endanger themselves by substituting fish that are harvested from polluted waters or beef that contains antibiotics or growth hormones.

By far the greatest threat to the food supply may be the use of pesticides and their effect on both the environment and the safety of the food consumed. In the late 1980's, apples treated

Consumers will need to fight for affordable housing. (Ron Sherman/Uniphoto)

with Alar (daminozide) — a growth regulator that also helped their skins retain their color — came under EPA scrutiny when it was linked with cancer. In March, 1989, the National Resources Defense Council (NRDC) cited Alar as the biggest threat to children's food, noting that one out of every four thousand children were at risk for cancer. There was a public outcry, and the media and consumer interest groups rallied to ban Alar. Although the carcinogenic properties of Alar were subsequently found to be much less dangerous than initially thought, the EPA established a schedule, beginning in September, 1989, to phase out Alar. Uniroyal Chemical Company suspended its U.S. sales of Alar by late 1989. By 1991, Alar was no longer being used on apple crops to regulate growth or in food processing, and it has been removed from the GRAS list. Nevertheless, apple growers and scientists alike were disillusioned by all the hoopla, and Washington State growers filed a lawsuit against the NRDC and the Columbia Broadcasting System for the way in which they had discredited the chemical.

Despite the assertion by the FDA that food treated with approved pesticides and other chemicals is safe, average consumers as well as consumer interest groups remain unconvinced. The increase in "organic" foods in the supermarket — foods grown without pesticides or other additives — testifies to this public concern. New techniques for genetically engineering crops show great promise but unknown consequences as well: Genetically engineered crops make it possible to breed plants that are resistant to pests and that produce greater yields, but there is concern among horticulturalists and naturalists (as well as some scientists) that plant varieties are disappearing. This could have negative effects on the ecological balance and the relationship between insects and plant life. In the twenty-first century, consumer activists will have their work cut out for them as they challenge domestic agricultural practices, as well as inspection procedures on imports, in an effort to secure greater safety with food consumption.

Electronic Shopping

Consumer issues of the future will address the distribution of goods. The current trend is toward shopping in megastores for convenience. In saving time and money, however, consumers may find themselves with fewer alternatives and a poor combination of price and quality. A conflict of consumer interest could result in changes in purchasing arrangements, such as laws that allow consumers to change their minds and cancel purchases, as is currently the case with door-to-door sales.

Another trend in distribution of goods is the increasing use of electronic or mail-order shopping. In recent surveys to measure consumer satisfaction, mail-order goods were high on the list of customer complaints. A study conducted by the Better Business Bureau found that store prices are almost always lower than a television shopping service's stated retail price. Electronic shopping also raises other issues, such as impulse buying, credit card fraud or theft, and access to personal information, as well as assigning responsibility when problems occur. Shopping over computer lines is also on the increase. No doubt consumers will need protection from unauthorized access as more people shop in this way.

High-Tech Throwaways?

In an era of rapid advancement, many new products are entering the marketplace, making it more challenging to make an informed decision. To complicate matters, as the price of new appliances goes down and the cost of repair goes up, the consumer is stuck with the dilemma of whether to buy a new VCR for $200 or to have the old one repaired for $150.

Unfortunately, serious quality problems have led to high repair costs not only for appliances but also for cars. The problem is complicated by the high cost of labor, which in turn is determined by two factors: inflation and a standard of living with high overheads. On the other hand, auto insurers claimed in 1989 that Americans were saving $388 million because they used auto parts that were cheaper imitations. As of 1992, Congress was considering the Design Protection Act, presented in 1991 by Representative Richard Gephardt of Missouri. This law would protect manufacturers from imitations. However, prices in sporting goods, packaged foods, and auto parts — to name only a few products — would probably rise if this law were passed.

Health and Auto Insurance

These two types of insurance are very much in need of reform. More and more families have inadequate health insurance or none at all. Senator Edward Kennedy has long been a supporter for a stronger social package on health

New Chemicals are always being tested on crops in an effort to meet government regulations, improve productivity, or to find chemicals that would be less harmful to the environment and the consumer. (Environmental Protection Agency)

insurance, but there has not been sufficient support from consumers as a whole and legislators to create a program for those families who do not qualify for Medicaid but are in need of more affordable health care.

Auto insurance rates are increasing yearly and appear to be beyond the control of the consumer. The recent rollbacks that insurers of California drivers were required to give were more than compensated for by the increase in rates. In particular, rates jump astronomically after an accident or when a moving violation goes on record. The increase in rates when an accident occurs is indicative of the inflated costs of auto repairs and health care. As the century draws to a close, these issues — health care and health and auto insurance — will need strong consumerist support to bring about changes that protect the already beleaguered consumer from ballooning costs.

Housing

The 1970's and the 1980's were the wonder years for real estate developers, even though the close of the 1980's brought with it a more depressed market. While many consumers have acquired personal gains through real estate transactions, more consumers have had to compromise in terms of both house and location. Other consumers have had to struggle each month just to come up with the rent, which increased because of the escalating house market. Owners who rent have also been hit hard. They face difficulties with quick turnover of renters as well as trying to juggle a high monthly mortgage payment with what is the acceptable rent for their area.

There is urgent need for housing that supports a growing segment of the consumer population: those who do not qualify for housing programs, such as the ones available through the U.S. Department of Housing and Urban Development (HUD), yet who find a single family home out of reach financially. What is currently available to the poor is not sufficient to meet

As Earth's population grows, so will the need for consumer protections. (S. C. Delaney/U.S. Environmental Protection Agency)

their needs, and the number of homeless persons is on the increase.

The Smart Consumer

The key to the strength of consumer interest groups is the education of consumers. Though consumers have become more sophisticated and knowledgeable, there is still much apathy among consumers. The average consumer is not action-oriented and would rather leave it to consumer interest groups or rely on government agencies to right a wrong.

Unfortunately, government agencies have even fewer resources since cutbacks in funding. The more that consumers educate themselves and advocate, the more likely there will be change. In the words of Ralph Nader, commenting on consumers of the 1990's:

> Consumers are more likely to complain in detail, more prone to know their rights — as with motor vehicle recalls and warranties — and more inclined to locate information that will help them defend themselves in the marketplace.

As the twenty-first century approaches, consumers must link consumer rights issues to other human rights issues — such as women's rights, children's rights, employment rights, and the rights of disabled persons — and look at consumer problems in a global context.

Time Line

1906   Pure Food and Drug Act. Guards against unsafe and treated food
        and drug products.
1906   Meat Inspection Act. Meat shipped from state to state has to be
        processed and packaged under sanitary conditions.
1914   Federal Trade Commission Act. Establishes the FTC. Declares
        "unfair methods of competition" to be illegal.
1938   Federal Food, Drug, and Cosmetic Act. Amends the act of 1906;
        includes cosmetics.
1953   Flammable Fabrics Act. Outlaws the manufacture or sale of clothing
        that is highly inflammable.
1958   Food Additives (Delaney) Amendment. Amends the act of 1938.
        Requires that only those foods or additives that do not cause cancer
        be "generally recognized as safe" for consumption.
1960   Hazardous Substances Labeling Act. Controls labeling of packages
        of hazardous household substances.
1962   Kefauver-Harris Amendments. Amends 1938 act, requiring all drugs
        to be both safe and effective.
1966   Cigarette Labeling and Advertising Act. Requires health warnings
        on cigarette packages.
1966   National Traffic and Motor Vehicle Safety Act. Establishes
        mandatory safety standards for automobiles and for new and used
        tires.
1966   Child Protection Act. Amends Hazardous Substances Labeling Act
        of 1960. Permits banning of hazardous substances; prevents
        marketing of potentially harmful toys and articles for children.
1968   Truth-in-Lending Act. Requires full disclosure of credit terms and
        conditions of finance charges in consumer credit transactions.
1968   Wholesome Poultry Products Act. Upgrades poultry inspection to
        meet federal standards.
1969   Child Protection and Toy Safety Act. Bans toys that pose electrical,
        fire, or mechanical hazards.
1970   Credit Card Liability Act. Limits credit card users to $50 liability if
        card is stolen or used without authorization.

1970   Fair Credit Reporting Act. Requires credit reporting companies to make reports available to consumers.

1970   Poison Prevention Packaging Act. Establishes standards for child-resistant closures on hazardous substances.

1972   Consumer Product Safety Act. Establishes Consumer Product Safety Commission with powers to set safety standards for broad range of consumer products.

1975   Energy Policy and Conservation Act. Requires manufacturers to label products with their energy consumption.

1975   Magnuson-Moss Warranty Act. Provides for consumer redress, including class action. Gives FTC extended powers to impose penalties for unfair or deceptive acts or practices.

1980   Infant Formula Act. Requires formula companies to label formula packages, stating the benefits of breast milk.

1984   Drug Price Competition and Patent Restoration Act. Hastens process by which generic drugs are approved by the FDA. Pharmacists can substitute generic for name-brand drugs.

1984   State seat-belt laws. States are required by the federal government to make their own seat-belt laws. The federal government provides funds for those states that enforce those laws.

1990   Clean Air Act Amendments. Provide guidelines for reducing emissions and air pollution between 50 and 75 percent under a two-year plan.

1991   Intermodal Surface Transportation Efficiency Act. Requires airbags to be included in all cars and trucks by September 1, 1997.

Publications

Barrett, Stephen, with the editors of *Consumer Reports*. *Health Schemes, Scams, and Frauds*. Mount Vernon, N.Y.: Consumers Union, 1990. This book claims to debunk what the authors identify as questionable health cures or medical interventions. Unfortunately, the subject is approached as if traditional medicine has all the right answers. While there is much useful questioning of such fads as weight-loss diets, there are many instances of bias on the part of the authors, such as their outright condemnation of chiropractors when many consumers have benefitted from them. For those who have been subjected to fraudulent practices in the health field, provides helpful resources and pointers on how to receive a fair hearing.

Caplovitz, David. *The Poor Pay More*. New York: Free Press, 1963. A classic. Examines low-income consumers in New York City and how they are discriminated against as consumers. This book was instrumental in bringing about reform in the use of credit.

Charell, Ralph. *Satisfaction Guaranteed: The Ultimate Guide to Consumer Self-Defense*. New York: Simon & Schuster, 1985. Strongly and unabashedly on the side of the consumer, this book is designed to empower consumers and give them some ammunition when negotiating with sellers. Written in a humorous vein, the sections on buying a car and the mail-order business are recommended.

Consumer Information Catalog. Washington, D.C.: Government Printing Office, quarterly. A free list of the federal government's best consumer pamphlets, covering topics from food and drugs to education, health, and investments.

Consumer Reports. Mount Vernon, N.Y.: Consumers Union. A monthly magazine that focuses on comparative product testing. There is much of practical value and general interest to consumers.

Consumer Sourcebook. 6th ed., edited by Robert Wilson. Detroit: Gale Research, 1990. An impressive and indispensable resource, listing consumer organizations and government agencies according to subject. Contains all the information consumers need to follow up on consumer interest activities, lodge a complaint, or learn their rights.

Crandall, Robert W., Howard K. Gruenspecht, Theodore E. Keeler, and Lester B. Lowe. *Regulating the Automobile*. Washington, D.C.: Brookings Institution, 1986. Examines the benefits and costs of three areas of automobile regulation: emissions control, fuel economy standards, and safety.

Dadd, Debra Lynn. *Nontoxic and Natural: A Guide for Consumers*. Los Angeles: Jeremy Tarcher, 1984. A resource book listing the known potentially toxic substances in products and their toxin-free alternatives. Covers a wide range of products, from food to water filters. A valuable resource for the ecologically minded and health-conscious consumer.

Dadd, Debra Lynn. *The Nontoxic Home*. Los Angeles: Jeremy Tarcher, 1986. A useful guide for the concerned consumer who wants safe alternatives to potentially harmful substances commonly found in the home. Includes, for example, information on how to minimize dangers from video display terminals.

Feldman, Lawrence P. *Consumer Protection*. New York: West Publishing, 1976. Although somewhat dated, a helpful book on how consumer protection has evolved during the twentieth century. It is detailed with plenty of valuable information; recommended for the more advanced reader.

Griffin, Kelley. *More Action for a Change*. New York: Dembner Books, 1987. Gives an account of Public Interest Research Groups (PIRGs), which were inspired by Nader. The appendix outlines how to start a PIRG.

Kallet, Arthur, and F. J. Schlink. *100,000,000 Guinea Pigs: Dangers in Everyday Foods, Drugs, and Cosmetics*. New York: Grosset & Dunlap, 1933. An indictment of companies that exposed consumers to untested products. Helped to bring about the Federal Food, Drug, and Cosmetic Act of 1938.

Mayer, Robert N. *The Consumer Movement: Guardians of the Marketplace*. Boston: Twayne, 1989. An excellent all-round account of the consumer movement and consumer rights, suitable for scholars. Covers all the relevant aspects of consumerism. This book provides a mixture of fact and insight into the development of the consumer movement during the past fifty years.

Mitford, Jessica. *The American Way of Death*. New York: Simon & Schuster, 1963. A classic that exposes how grieving relatives are subjected to unreasonable pressure by the funeral industry.

Nader, Ralph. *Beware*. New York: Meilen Press, 1971. An introduction to consumer advocacy, this book gives many examples of how household products have been unsafe. The purpose of *Beware* is to prevent injury and death of consumers, and although it is now dated, it provides noteworthy accounts of companies violating safety regulations. The book will encourage consumers to question whatever they buy and not to believe in so-called trusted names. Nader shows, for example, that the "Good Housekeeping" seal does not protect consumers as much as the public has been led to believe.

Nader, Ralph. *Unsafe at Any Speed*. New York: Grossman, 1965. Exposed the irresponsibilities of the American automotive industry, and helped bring about the Highway Safety Act in 1966. Nader called into question how the interiors of cars did not protect passengers in a collision, and in particular pointed out problems with the then-popular Corvair. This book made Nader a household name and figurehead of the consumer movement.

Nader, Ralph, and William Taylor. *The Big Boys*. New York: Pantheon, 1986. Profiles of corporate executives, such as Roger Smith of General Motors, which are not altogether unfavorable. Some Nader supporters fear he has "gone soft" in this book.

Sinclair, Upton. *The Jungle*. New York: Doubleday Page, 1906. Describes the life of a fictionalized immigrant family who try to earn a living in Chicago's slaughterhouses at the beginning of the twentieth century. An indictment of the system, hoping to elicit sympathy for socialism from the reader, this book proved to be the first exposé pointing to the need for consumer rights.

Media Resources

Adlon, Percy, and Eleonor Adlon, producers. *Rosalie Goes Shopping*, 1989. Film, available in video. Distributed by Vidmark Entertainment. A satire that alludes to the darker side of credit transactions and electronic shopping. Armed with a computer and a bogus company, Rosalie (Marianne Sägebrecht) goes on a shopping spree that threatens bankruptcy — that is, until she finds ways to generate more and more credit.

Ardi, Dana, and Theo Mayer, producers. *Automotive Repair for Dummies: The Maintenance Tape*, 1987. Video. Distributed by McGraw-Hill and Metavision. Gives the viewer many easy-to-follow suggestions for keeping a car in good condition. Based on consumer expert Deanne Sclar's book of the same name.

Backstreet Studios and Cambridge Career Products, producers. *Surviving the Checkout: Wise Food Buying*, 1990. Video. Distributed by the producers. Although the acting is amateurish, the information is useful to the beginning shopper. Accompanied by a workbook.

Consumer Reports, producer. *Consumer Reports*, 1987. Video. Distributed by Warner Home Video. A series on how to consume wisely. Includes information on cars, houses, traveling, investing, and burglar-proofing the home.

Dallas County Community College, producer. *Ralph Nader: Opinion Leader*, 1979. Video. Distributed by the producer. Focuses on consumer advocate Ralph Nader and how he rose to his position as a national opinion leader and activist.

Fight Back! David Horowitz, a consumer advocate, hosts this television program aired by the National Broadcasting Company (NBC). He addresses consumer interests and complaints. A significant feature of the program is testing claims made by manufacturers in television commercials.

Herbal Life International, producer. *For Your Family's Sake*, 1988. Video. Distributed by the producer. Documents illness and deaths of children that have been linked to contaminated water. Takes a hard look at the quality of tap water and its potential dangers.

Herriott, Steven A., producer. *The Smart Buyer's Guide to Purchasing a New Car*, 1991. Video. Distributed by Alexander Media Services. This video is what unscrupulous automobile dealers hope consumers never see. The straightforward presentation offers concise, well-rounded coverage of useful facts to know before buying a car.

KCET/PBS, producer. *Diet for a New America: Your Planet, Your Choice*, 1991. Available from KCET Video, 4401 Sunset Blvd., Los Angeles, CA 90027. Watched by one million viewers in its first airing on KCET in Los Angeles, this video is a journey into the great American food machine. Reveals the dramatic impact of people's daily food choices on the body's health as well as the environment.

Little, Dave, producer. *How to Buy a Used Car*, 1989. Video. Distributed by Meridian Education Corporation. Gives teenage viewers a clear idea of the ins and outs of buying a used car. The most successful scene shows the actual inspection of a used car.

Magna Systems, producer. *Consumer Education*, 1988. Videos. Distributed by producer. A series of videotapes on the history of consumerism and consumer-related topics, such as clothing, real estate, and buying a car.

Moore, Michael, producer. *Roger and Me*, 1989. Film, available in video. Distributed by Warner Home Video. A hard-hitting documentary on how the town of Flint, Michigan, attempts to survive the crippling effects of the General Motors layoff of thirty thousand workers in 1986. Michael Moore relentlessly pursues Roger Smith of General Motors for an interview, and so exposes the ruthless edge of the automotive industry.

National Safety Council, producer. *Consumer Fraud: Games Con Men Play*, 1981. Video. Distributed by Aims Media. A fifteen-minute video on the unethical selling practices of mail-order and easy-credit schemes.

Nichols, Mike, producer. *Silkwood*, 1983. Film, available in video. Distributed by Nelson. The story of Karen Silkwood, a nuclear power plant worker and activist, who mysteriously died in a car crash in 1974. Just before the accident, Silkwood was on her way to tell a reporter about safety violations in the Kerr-McGhee Cimarron plutonium plant outside Oklahoma City, where she worked.

Public Policy Productions for WNET. *Energy Efficiency, Parts 1 and 2*, 1986. Shows how great a part the latest improvements in energy efficiency can play in meeting society's energy needs.

Organizations
and
Hotlines

Consumer Federation of America
1424 Sixteenth St. NW, Suite 604
Washington, DC 20036
(202) 387-6121
   Consumer Federation of America seeks to advance pro-consumer policy
in legislatures and the courts; it acts as a clearinghouse for the exchange of
consumer information, ideas, and experiences. Committees of CFA address
such issues as communications, credit, education, energy, the environment,
food, health, housing, insurance, political action, taxation, transportation,
and the needs of low-income consumers.

Consumer Information Center
General Services Administration
18th and F Streets NW
Washington, DC 20405
(202) 501-1794
   A leading source of printed information for the American consumer, on
the federal level. Publishes the *Consumer Information Catalog*, available
free from the Consumer Information Center, Pueblo, CO 81009.

Consumer Product Safety Commission
Office of Information and Public Affairs
Washington, DC 20207
(301) 504-0580
(800) 638-CPSC (hotline)
   This agency was established to protect consumers. It enforces federal
laws regulating a wide variety of products. The National Injury Information

Clearinghouse, at (301) 504-0424, is a division of the CPSC which disseminates information on unreasonable injury.

Consumers Union of the United States
101 Truman Ave.
Yonkers, NY 10703-1057
(914) 378-2000
   Probably best known for its monthly magazine *Consumer Reports*, which tests, reviews, and compares a wide variety of different consumer goods. This organization's Used Car Price Service can be consulted by calling (900) 446-0500, which gives current prices, estimated regionally, for used vehicles of approximately the previous decade. There is a toll for the call, which is quoted at the beginning of a taped message.

Council of Better Business Bureaus
Auto Line Program
4200 Wilson Blvd., Suite 800
Arlington, VA 22203
(703) 276-0100
   Uses mediation and arbitration to settle disputes between consumers and the auto industry. State offices.

Department of Housing and Urban Development
451 Seventh St. SW
Washington, DC 20410
(202) 708-0980
(800) 699-9777 (housing discrimination hotline)
   HUD is the principal federal agency for programs concerned with housing needs, fair housing, and community development.

Environmental Protection Agency
Public Information Center
401 M St. SW
Washington, DC 20460
(202) 260-7751
   Provides information and sponsors programs on environmental issues. Regional offices.

Federal Trade Commission
Bureau of Consumer Protection

Sixth St. and Pennsylvania Ave. NW
Washington, DC 20580
(202) 326-3238; consumer inquiries hotline, (202) 326-2222
     The FTC was established to prevent the use of unfair or deceptive
advertising and marketing practices.

Food and Drug Administration
Office of Consumer Affairs
5600 Fishers Lane, Room 16-63
Rockville, MD 20857
(301) 443-3170
     This office serves as a consumer information source for food- and drug-
related subjects, including FDA regulations, general drug information,
medical devices, and health fraud.

The Housing Advocates, Inc.
3214 Prospect Ave., East
Cleveland, OH 44115-2600
(216) 431-5300
     Founded in 1975, this organization promotes equal housing
opportunities and advocates safe, good-quality housing for low-income
families.

National Highway Traffic Safety Administration
Department of Transportation
400 Seventh St. SW
Washington, DC 20590
(202) 366-0123, (800) 424-9393 (auto safety hotlines)
     NHTSA was established to reduce automobile injuries and deaths. The
agency provides financial and technical assistance to states and works
closely with private organizations to improve road safety. The hotline
provides information on crash test results, car recalls, and car defects.
There are ten regional offices.

National Safety Council
1121 Spring Lake Dr.
Itasca, IL 60143
     A nongovernmental, nonprofit organization devoted to educating the
public to adopt safety and health policies and to prevent accidents. Provides
both free information and publications and videos on sale.

Public Citizen
P.O. Box 19404
Washington, DC 20036
(202) 833-3000
Founded in 1971 by Ralph Nader, Public Citizen represents consumers through lobbying, litigation, research, and publications. The organization has been successful in getting the FDA to ban unsafe drugs.

TRW National Consumer Relations Center
12606 Greenville Ave.
Dallas, TX 75354
(214) 235-1200, ext. 251
Provides information about credit reporting centers, credit law, and one free credit report annually.

INDEX